THE LAWSUIT HANDBOOK

RICHARD COOMBS, ESQ.

LAWPREP PRESS, CALIFORNIA

LawPrep Press, Inc., a
California corporation

© 1990 by

LawPrep Press
17900 North Sky Park Circle
Suite 100
Irvine, California 92714

Printed in the United States of America

THE LAWSUIT HANDBOOK

This book is designed to assist you in understanding the litigation process. The book explores the various stages of litigation from pre-trial through appeals. The costs of litigation are carefully examined as are the issues you will encounter while in the court system. This book will help you better understand and survive the litigation process with the assistance of an attorney.

CONTENTS

INTRODUCTION

The legal system in the United States is a forum for citizens who seek a remedy for an injury or wrong. This applies whether someone loses the use of a car, suffers some personal injury, loses money based on bad advice or is precluded from exercising some personal freedom to which that person believes he or she is entitled. Most people believe that the courts are the guardians of these rights and are more willing to resort to the courts to protect these rights. Most Americans, however, do not have a thorough understanding of the internal operations and procedures of the courts and the American legal system.

If a dispute exists between people that cannot be resolved by agreement, most Americans are aware that they are entitled to their day in court. When most Americans are involved in a lawsuit, however, they become extremely frustrated at the time and expense involved in a process that does not operate by the same rules as they use in their everyday lives.

There are three major factors which distinguish the legal system from the way most people conduct their lives. First, there is the structure. Courts have strict time requirements and strict rules regarding how one makes a claim, in what forum that claim can be made, the specific format necessary to make the claim, what can be said in court, how it can be said, and even when it can be said.

Second, the system is operated by judges and lawyers. Judges and lawyers are highly educated people. That is not to say that they have any greater natural intelligence or common sense but they have spent several years learning how to "think like a lawyer." Thinking like a lawyer, as every first year law school student must learn, is different from the way people normally think. It is analytical and logical in the extreme, and the focus of the analysis and logic is details, not necessarily general concepts. This leads us to the third factor that differentiates the legal system.

Courts do not base decisions upon the presentation of general concepts or upon synopses of events. Courts require the preservation of raw data, the details from which they reach conclusions. This is probably the reason that so many people find the logic of judges and lawyers illogical. Whereas most people can logically analyze a situation, lawyers and judges must concentrate and apply their analyses to details of the situation that may seem unimportant or irrelevant to the general public. The reason that these details are important is because the Rules of Law say that they are important.

The Rules of Law derive from two sources: (1) the legislature; and (2) evolution over the years by court decisions. These Rules of Law must be specific to be enforceable and are fact specific. That is, that different Rules of Law apply to different fact patterns. Therefore, lawyers and judges must strictly apply the specific Rules of Law to the specific facts that are presented as evidence in each case.

The purpose of this book is not to be an apologist for the legal system. I am a lawyer, I work in the legal system, and I believe in the legal system, but it has significant problems and can be markedly improved. Those problems and possible improvements are beyond the scope of this book.

This book, rather, is a guidebook or a map. Most litigants are very result oriented. They know exactly what result they want and often are not concerned with how that result is achieved. The legal system is very process oriented. It is less concerned with the result than it is with the way that the result is reached. The process is complex, somewhat cumbersome and foreign to most people. This book is my effort to assist you in understanding the process.

One of the biggest fears among litigants is the fear of the unknown. If you can understand the process, you may be able to better appreciate the time and money necessary to proceed with a lawsuit. If deciding whether to begin a lawsuit, this book will provide valuable information that will help you make a more reasoned decision. If you find yourself already in a lawsuit, especially as a defendant, this should help you understand what is involved in the legal process.

CHAPTER 1

COURT SYSTEMS

The best place to start a book on the process of litigation is with a brief description of the various courts in the United States. The courts constitute the branch of government that are charged with arbitrating disputes. They also constitute the branch of government that is least understood. The court system is often thought of as a large and impersonal monolith. Actually, though, there are several different court systems, and within each system, there are several levels of courts. Each of these courts follows different procedures and applies different rules of law.

The reason for this variety is that this country is composed of fifty different states, each with its own legislature which has passed its own laws to be enforced in that state, and each with its own court system which has established its own rules. In addition to the states, the United States government has its own laws passed by Congress and its own court system. All of these courts, in all states and at all levels, exist for one primary purpose; they exist to resolve disputes among people that cannot be otherwise peaceably resolved. Criminal trials can be included in this purpose, since a criminal trial involves a dispute between the government and the defendant. For our purposes, however, we will focus on civil matters.

Several of these court systems, especially in metropolitan areas, can be quite large. It is inaccurate to consider the courts as monolithic, however. You may be surprised at the disagreements among judges between different court systems and even within the same court system. Even though nearly all court proceedings are open to the public and press, most court proceedings do not generate much interest, so most court business is conducted without observers or publicity.

Courts are the least political of the branches of government. Even where judges are elected, those elections generally do not revolve around political issues unless there has been a particularly unpopular decision that has been highly publicized. Most judges at some time must make public policy decisions, but at the trial court level, those decisions affect only the parties to the lawsuit. Therefore, the public is not generally privy to the political haggling and argument among judges.

But make no mistake, courts are not a single system with one approach. Each court system can, and does, make decisions different from other court systems, and within each court system, each judge has his or her own interpretation. Serious legal arguments often occur between different courts, sometimes even within the same court system, but those arguments occur in well reasoned, scholarly decisions that are bound in volumes rather than argued in the popular press.

While courts may seem impersonal, they are actually both personal and impersonal. They are the most personal branch of government in that every matter handled by the courts is a dispute between people. The vast majority of cases do not involve any issues of public interest. Therefore, the judicial branch is the only branch of government that deals, almost exclusively, with the problems which exist between differing individuals.

Courts are perceived as impersonal for two main reasons. One is that, even though they decide personal disputes, the courts seldom decide those disputes based upon which position evokes more empathy. Every trial

7

lawyer can point to some exceptions to that statement, but generally, courts decide these personal disputes based upon the rules of law and only a comprehensive study of laws and how they are applied can make you more comfortable with the Rules of Law. Therefore, the purpose of this book is to increase your awareness of the legal process and its internal rules and procedures.

In this chapter, we will examine the various court systems and the different levels of trial courts within those systems. Trial courts have what is known as original jurisdiction. Trial courts are the first tier for dispute resolution. They are the courts in which you file an initial lawsuit. These courts conduct trials. Not all courts have original jurisdiction. Most appellate courts do not conduct trials. Rather, they hear appeals and writs filed usually by the person who lost in the trial court to overturn a lower court ruling or decision. Except under certain limited circumstances, appellate courts do not have original jurisdiction and do not conduct trials. This book will focus on trial courts, because they are the only courts in which witnesses generally appear and the only courts in which individuals, other than lawyers, actually participate in the legal process.

FEDERAL COURTS

Appellate Courts

The United States Supreme Court is the only court established by the United States Constitution. All other courts in the federal system have been created by Congress. The Supreme Court is the court of last resort in the United States. The justices of the Supreme Court decide which cases they will review. Many of their decisions have far reaching consequences, since every citizen and state is subject to their rulings. The Supreme Court is an appellate court. It has original jurisdiction only in cases affecting Ambassadors, other public ministers and Consuls and certain cases in which a state is a party.

The Congress has established Courts of Appeal. The country is divided into several circuits each with its own court of appeal. If someone appeals a decision rendered by a federal trial court, that appeal proceeds to the Court of Appeal that covers the particular trial court in which the decision was made. For example, if a decision is made by the trial court in the Eastern District of California, the appeal would be to the Ninth Circuit Court of Appeal. The

9

Ninth Circuit includes California, eight other western states and Guam.

U.S. District Courts.

Every state, the District of Columbia and Puerto Rico has at least one federal district court, officially known as the United States District Courts. The district courts are the trial courts within the federal court system. Only certain cases may be brought to a federal district court for resolution. Article III, Section 2 of the United States Constitution provides that federal courts have jurisdiction only in the following cases: all cases arising under the Constitution, federal laws or treaties; all cases involving Ambassadors, other public ministers and Consuls; admiralty and maritime cases; cases in which the United States is a party; cases arising between states; those between a state and citizens of a different state; cases between citizens of different states; cases arising between citizens of one state claiming lands under a grant from a different state; and those cases between a state or its citizens and a foreign government or its citizens.

Many of the circumstances which provide for federal jurisdiction do not occur often. It is not customary to hear

10

claims by citizens of one state regarding lands under a grant issued by another state. It is also unlikely that many of you are Ambassadors or Consuls. So the most likely way that you might be in federal court is in cases involving federal laws or under what is known as diversity jurisdiction. Diversity jurisdiction means that a federal court has the authority to hear a dispute if all of the parties are citizens of different states. This is true even if the issues in the lawsuit do not involve any federal questions, if each party to the lawsuit resides in a different state and as long as certain other criteria that Congress has established are satisfied, then a case may be tried in a federal district court.

The federal courts have the right to declare an act of Congress or a regulation passed by the government unconstitutional. Since the United States Constitution, federal laws and treaties are supreme to state law, the federal courts can also declare any act of a state or any provision of a state constitution to be invalid because it conflicts with the United States Constitution or federal law.

There is at least one district court in each federal district. In some instances a federal district has the same boundaries as a state, such as the District of Kansas. Federal districts, however, are not necessarily the same as a state. California, for example, has four federal districts. Since federal judges have the authority to render decisions

11

as they deem appropriate, they have lifetime tenure, and can be removed only by impeachment, federal judges are among the most powerful people in our government. That power is moderated since federal judges do not choose the issues on which they rule; they only rule on the issues presented to them in a lawsuit.

FEDERAL CIRCUITS AND DISTRICT COURTS[1]
(The number of circuit and district judges is shown in parenthesis)

CIRCUIT (Appellate Courts)	DISTRICTS (Trial Courts)
District of Columbia (12)	District of Columbia(15)
First (6)	Maine (2) Massachusetts (10) New Hampshire (2) Puerto Rico (7) Rhode Island (2)
Second (13)	Connecticut (5) New York --Northern (3) --Southern (27) --Eastern (10) --Western (3) Vermont (2)
Third (12)	Delaware (3) New Jersey (11) Pennsylvania --Eastern (19) --Middle (5)

---

[1]The information in this chart is compiled from 28 United States Code Service, Sections 41, 44 and 133.

--Western (10)
Virgin Islands *

Fourth (11)

Maryland (9)
North Carolina
--Eastern (3)
--Western (3)
--Middle (3)
South Carolina (8)
Virginia
--Eastern (8)
--Western (4)
West Virginia
--Northern (2)
--Southern (4)

Fifth (16)

District of the Canal Zone
Louisiana
--Eastern (13)
--Middle (2)
--Western (5)
Mississippi
--Northern (2)
--Southern (3)

Texas

--Northern (9)
--Southern (13)
--Eastern (4)
--Western (6)

14

Sixth (15)

Kentucky
--Eastern (4)
--Western (3)
--Eastern and Western (1)
Michigan
--Eastern (13)
--Western (4)
Ohio
--Northern (9)
--Southern (6)
Tennessee
--Eastern (3)
--Middle (3)
--Western (3)

Seventh (11)

Illinois
--Northern (16)
--Central (3)
--Southern (2)
Indiana
--Northern (4)
--Southern (5)
Wisconsin
--Eastern (4)
--Western (2)

Eighth (10)

Arkansas
--Eastern (3)
--Western (1)
--Eastern and Western (2)

Iowa
--Northern (1)
--Southern (2)
--Northern and Southern (1)
Minnesota (5)
Missouri
--Eastern (4)
-Western (5)
-Eastern and Western (2)
Nebraska (3)
North Dakota (2)
South Dakota (3)

Ninth (28)

Alaska (2)
Arizona (8)
California
--Northern (12)
--Eastern (6)
--Central (17)
--Southern (7)
Guam *
Hawaii (2)
Idaho (2)
Montana (2)
Nevada (3)
Oregon (5)
Washington
--Eastern (2)
--Western (5)

Tenth (10)

Colorado (6)
Kansas (5)
New Mexico (4)
Oklahoma
--Northern (2)
--Eastern (1)
--Western (3)
--Northern, Eastern and
  Western (2)
Utah (3)
Wyoming (1)

Eleventh (12)

Alabama
--Northern (7)
--Middle (3)
--Southern (2)
Florida
--Northern (3)
--Middle (9)
--Southern (12)
Georgia
--Northern (11)
--Middle (2)
--Southern (3)

Federal (12)

All federal districts

17

STATE COURTS

Before examining the state courts, it is important to understand the difference between matters of law and matters of equity. Matters of law are those in which one party is suing for some type of compensation; the plaintiff, the person who initiates the lawsuit, wants compensation for some loss or damage.

Matters of equity, however, are those in which the court orders a person to perform, or not perform, a particular act. For example, an eviction case is a matter of equity, because the court has the power to remove a defendant, the person who is sued, from his home. Equity is often used to force someone to perform under a contract or to cease engaging in a wrongful act.

Appellate Courts

Every state has a supreme court which is the highest court in that state, although New York refers to this court as the Court of Appeals. The supreme court is, in all states except one, primarily an appellate court. Some supreme courts have limited original jurisdiction granted by state constitutions or laws. Maine's supreme court, known as the Supreme Judicial Court, has original jurisdiction over all equity matters.

Most states have a tier of appellate courts between the trial courts and the supreme courts. There are a few states - for example, Nebraska, Nevada and New Hampshire - that do not. In most cases where these courts exist, they handle the appeals directly from the trial courts. Only under unusual circumstances can cases proceed directly from a trial court to a supreme court. One example is death penalty rulings which, in some states, may be appealed directly to the state supreme court.

General Jurisdiction Courts

All states and territories have a general jurisdiction trial court. Most states also have some limited jurisdiction courts and specialty courts. For our purposes, since we are primarily interested in civil lawsuits, we will refer to limited jurisdiction courts as those that are authorized to hear cases involving disputes only up to a certain dollar limit. Specialty courts are carved out of the court system to handle certain specified types of matters. A general jurisdiction court may handle any case which arises in its state or county and is the main trial court which handles civil cases.

Seventeen states refer to their general jurisdiction courts as Superior Courts (although Indiana's Superior Court shares its general jurisdiction with Indiana's Circuit Court. Pennsylvania's Superior Court has no original jurisdiction).

Eighteen states have Circuit Courts which are their general jurisdiction courts. Utah's Circuit Court is a limited jurisdiction court that may not handle cases involving more than claims for $10,000. New York's court of general jurisdiction is its Supreme Court. Maine's Supreme Judicial Court is a general jurisdiction court that only hears matters of equity.

Some trial courts hear only matters of law, and others hear only matters of equity. However, most cases are matters of law. The distinction between law and equity is rooted in several hundred years of American and English legal history. Although it has diminished in importance over the years, it remains a firmly established distinction. If a litigant seeks a judgment for money damages, that is a request for a legal remedy. But if the claim is for performance or non-performance of an act, that is a

20

request for an equitable remedy. Many cases involve both legal and equitable issues, so that under modern law, most state courts hear both issues.

Arkansas, Delaware and Mississippi have Chancery Courts which are general jurisdiction courts that hear only equity matters. Tennessee's Chancery Court is a general jurisdiction court hearing both law and equity matters, but its Circuit Court also has general jurisdiction for matters of law. Mississippi's Circuit Court also hears only legal matters. Other courts that hear only legal - and not equitable - matters are Massachusetts' District Court and the Superior Courts of Delaware and Maine. For all of their differences, and regardless of the names by which they are known, these are the main trial courts in the state court systems.

Limited Jurisdiction Courts

Many, but not all, states have limited jurisdiction courts. These courts often hear the same types of cases that general jurisdiction courts hear, but they can hear civil cases only if the amount in dispute is no higher than a certain dollar amount. The jurisdictional limit for most of these courts ranges from $10,000 to $25,000, although

Vermont's District Court is limited to $5,000, and Alaska's District Court is limited to $35,000.

Just as general jurisdiction courts are known by a number of names, so are limited jurisdiction courts. Some of these names are: Circuit Court (Utah); Common Pleas (Arkansas and Delaware); County Courts (11 states); Justice Courts (6 states); and Municipal Courts (6 states). The District Court has different jurisdictions in various states. In fifteen states, District Courts are limited jurisdiction courts. In another fifteen, District Courts are general jurisdiction courts. Then there is Rhode Island whose District Courts have limited jurisdiction only as to legal matters. In Massachusetts, the District Court is both a court of general and limited jurisdiction - general as to legal matters and limited as to equitable matters.

In the handling of criminal matters, you will often find that the limited jurisdiction courts, if they have jurisdiction to hear criminal matters at all, will hear the misdemeanor or more minor criminal trials, and the general jurisdiction courts will hear the more serious felonies. In civil matters, it is the courts of limited jurisdiction that hear the smaller matters and can often handle them more quickly and efficiently than the general jurisdiction courts.

Small Claims Courts

In a few states, small claims courts are separate courts. In most states, however, small claims are handled as a division of another court, often the limited jurisdiction court. A few states have no separate small claims courts or divisions. Small claims courts handle the very smallest of claims. The jurisdictional limits for small claims courts range from $1,000 to $5,000 depending on the state law.

The main distinction between small claims courts and other trial courts is that most states do not allow attorneys to represent parties in small claims matters. Small claims courts are the true People's Courts. Small claims courts are inexpensive for the parties, and rulings are made quickly. There is an important drawback in many small claims courts which is that the party who brings a claim may not appeal if he or she loses, but the one who is sued may appeal an adverse decision.

Specialty Courts

Many court systems also have specialty courts while other states either do not separately handle these specialty areas or handle them as a division of another court. For example, some states have separate probate courts or juvenile courts, while other states have these functions handled as divisions within their general jurisdiction courts. Although the Municipal Court is a limited jurisdiction court in some states, such as Arkansas and Ohio, it is a specialty court in other states, such as Alabama and Texas. In those states, the Municipal Court usually handles only cases involving breaches of local ordinances.

The names and types of specialty courts are as varied as the perceived local needs. Among the most notable specialty courts are police courts, tax courts, courts of conciliation, county courts, courts of claims, orphans courts, housing courts, land courts, justice courts, surrogates courts, family courts and mayor's courts. Since these courts have narrow jurisdictions, they will not be covered in this book.

GENERAL JURISDICTION AND LIMITED JURISDICTION
STATE TRIAL COURTS[2]

(NOTE: This list does not include courts that are authorized for only one county or city.)

STATE	GENERAL JURISDICTION (COURTS)	LIMITED JURISDICTION (COURTS)
Alabama	Circuit	District
Alaska	Superior	District
		Magistrate
Arizona	Superior	Justice
Arkansas	Circuit	-----
	Chancery (Equity)	
California	Superior	Municipal
Colorado	District	County
Connecticut	Superior	-----
Delaware (Law)	Chancery (Equity)	Common Pleas
	Superior (Law)	
District of Columbia	Superior	-----

---

[2]The information in this chart was compiled from Martindale-Hubbell Law Directory, Vol VIII, Law Digest, 1990.

Florida	Circuit	County
Georgia	Superior	-----
	State (Law)	
Hawaii	Circuit	District
Idaho	District	-----
Illinois	Circuit	-----
Indiana	Superior	County
	Circuit	
Iowa	District	----- *
Kansas	District	----- *
Kentucky	Circuit	District
Louisiana	District	Parrish
		City
		Justice of the Peace
Maine	Supreme Judicial	District
	(Equity)	
	Superior	
Maryland	Circuit	District (Law)
Massachusetts	Superior	District
Michigan	Circuit	District
Minnesota	District	County
Mississippi	Circuit (Law)	County
	Chancery (Equity)	
Missouri	Circuit	-----
Montana	District	Justice of the Peace
Nebraska	District	County
Nevada	District	Justices'
New Hampshire	Superior	District
New Jersey	Superior	Municipal
New Mexico	District	Magistrate

New York	Supreme	County
		District
North Carolina	Superior	District
North Dakota	District	County
Ohio	Common Pleas	Municipal
		County
Oklahoma	District	-----
Oregon	Circuit	District
Pennsylvania	Common Pleas	District
Puerto Rico	Superior	District
Rhode Island	Superior	District (Law)
South Carolina	Circuit (also called Common Pleas)	-----
South Dakota	Circuit	-----
Tennessee	Chancery (Equity)	Justice of the Peace
	Circuit (Law)	General Sessions
Texas	District	County Justices'
Utah	District	Circuit
Vermont	Superior	District
Virgin Islands	U.S. District Court	Territorial
Virginia	Circuit	-----
Washington	Superior	District
		Municipal
West Virginia	Circuit	County Magistrates'
Wisconsin	Circuit	-----
Wyoming	District	Justices'

* Commissioners or magistrates of the general jurisdiction court have limited jurisdiction.

Alternative Dispute Resolution

Alternative dispute resolution ("ADR") is a generic term used to describe methods of resolving disputes by means other than by a trial in court. Sometimes ADR is incorporated into the court systems, such as with court ordered mandatory arbitration. More often, however, it is voluntarily undertaken by the parties to a dispute.

In some states, ADR is an informal method for resolving disputes while in other states, especially in areas where the courts are quite congested, ADR is viewed as a means to alleviate the over-burdened court system.

ADR will be examined in further detail later in the book. For now, it is important to know that there are two basic types of ADR: (1) Mediation, in which an independent third party resolves a dispute; this method is popular in the area of labor relations; and (2) Arbitration, in which an arbitrator makes a decision. Both parties to a dispute need to consent to arbitration and determine whether it will be binding or merely advisory.

CHAPTER 2

REQUIREMENTS FOR A LAWSUIT

Lawsuits do not just fall out of the sky and attack someone. Most people who are sued feel that the person suing them has no justification for including them in the lawsuit, and sometimes they are right. Some people do file lawsuits without justification and will include as many people as possible, including those who have little or no reason to be included in the lawsuit. It is a fairly common practice to involve as many people as possible to increase the pool from which a settlement may be paid. Even if a plaintiff is not trying to maximize the potential settlement pool, he or she will often include many defendants simply because, at the early stages of a proceeding, he or she may not know the exact role of certain parties in the alleged claims.

All of this may seem eminently unfair to someone who becomes a defendant in a lawsuit that he or she knows little about or thinks is not justified. American tradition zealously protects a person's right to take his or her grievances to court. In most cases, there is no requirement that an effort to resolve a dispute be made before a lawsuit is filed. However, there are certain prerequisites to filing a lawsuit. There can be no lawsuit unless there has been some type of relationship between the plaintiff and the defendant and some dispute has arisen from that relationship. In most cases, the plaintiff will have suffered some injury or damage for which he or she is seeking compensation; in others, he or she will be seeking equity so that he will not suffer some damage due to some actual or threatened act by the defendant.

Let us examine in detail the requirements that must be satisfied before a lawsuit may be filed: a relationship; a dispute arising out of that relationship; and a need by the plaintiff for either compensation or protection.

RELATIONSHIP

Every contact creates a relationship. Every relationship involves expectations and obligations, including the performance of some duties. The fulfillment of expectations and duties is dependant upon the type of relationship and the generally understood rules applicable to that type of relationship.

Contract

Every contract creates a relationship. Contracts can be either written or oral. A written contract is best since it sets forth the understood rules of any relationship. Therefore, the expectations and duties are clearly established and, hopefully, easy to interpret.

The law imposes certain duties in every contractual relationship. For example, there is an implied duty to act in good faith and not act in a manner that would make it more difficult or impossible for the other person to fulfill his or her duties under the terms of the contract.

For example, if you contracted to purchase one million specially-cut carrot sticks and you want to be relieved of your duty to purchase the carrots, but you do not want to breach your contract, because then you will have to pay damages for your breach of contract. In order to be relieved of your obligation to purchase carrots, you may not convince the grower not to supply the carrots, if you do, you will have breached the contract, for interfering with the seller's ability to perform, i.e., deliver the carrots.

Oral contracts, contracts that are not in writing, are legal and binding in most cases. The problem with oral contracts is that it is difficult to determine what the obligations and duties of each party are under the terms of the contract. At the beginning of a relationship, the parties may have the same goals and expectations, but after awhile, they realize that each of them expected different results. If one blames the other for his or her failed expectations, then a court may have to decide the duties of each person, and all the court can use to make this decision is the oral testimony of each of the parties since there is no written document to introduce into evidence. Many misunderstandings arise from oral contracts, because they often are not as detailed as written contracts and because the parties do not have a clear understanding of what their rights and duties are under the contract.

Certain types of contracts must be in writing to be binding. Historically, this requirement applied to: (a) contracts that could not be performed within one year; (b) contracts for the sale of an interest in real property; (c) contracts entered into in contemplation of marriage; (d) contracts for the sale of goods over $500.00; and (e) contracts to pay the debt of another (i.e., a guarantee).

The states have modified this list, but nearly every state has some statute that has similar requirements. These statutes are called the statutes of frauds.

Personal

Strictly personal relationships are also the genesis for a lawsuit. Generally, the more intense the personal relationship, the greater the possibility for a lawsuit. Marriage is probably the most likely personal relationship to give rise to a lawsuit usually for divorce or dissolution of the marriage. This is not a purely personal relationship, in a legal sense, because for years the courts treated divorces as breach of contract cases. With the arrival of no-fault divorces over the past few years, marriage is viewed as a personal relationship that is ending rather than as a contract that has been breached. However, remnants of the contractual view of marriage remain.

Parents of children have duties to each other and to the children regardless of whether the parents are married to each other. These duties give rise to claims for child support and lawsuits to determine the father of a child (a paternity lawsuit).

Fiduciary

Fiduciary relationships, also known as trust relationships, are very special relationships in which one person has fiduciary duties to the other and owes the other a high degree of trust and care.

Fiduciary relationships may be created by agreement or by law. A trustee named in a trust agreement has a fiduciary duty to protect the trust property for the benefit of all beneficiaries of the trust. An executor or administrator of an estate or the conservator for an incompetent person all have fiduciary duties that are created by law. Because of the need for insurance and the financial strength of insurance companies, many states consider insurers to have fiduciary duties to their insured.

Duties To The Public

The duties that you owe to the public in general vary from state to state depending upon the criminal and negligence laws in each state. Most crimes are considered a breach of an obligation either to the state or to the people of the state. Since we are not concentrating on criminal matters in this book, we can say that, in general, you have a duty to the public to act carefully so as not to cause any other member of the public physical harm or loss. This is often called negligence.

Claims of negligence can arise in many different kinds of relationships, but your duties to the public give rise to the numerous lawsuits over traffic accidents. While you may believe that you have no "relationship" with another driver on the roadway, you do. If you drive negligently and injure that driver or damage his car, you can be sued for damages by the owner or driver of the car. One step farther removed from traditional ideas of a "relationship" are the lawsuits brought by the family of the driver who was killed through the careless or negligent driving of another.

Indirect Relationship

It is possible for you to be named in another person's lawsuit even when you have tried to comply with your duties and obligations. For example, if you build a house on a lot you own, you may have to prepare an environmental impact report ("EIR") setting forth how your project will affect the environment and what efforts you will make to mitigate any negative impacts on the environment.

The city will tell you what needs to be in the EIR, and usually you will hire a professional to prepare it. The city will then consider and vote on your EIR. If the city approves your EIR, you may proceed with your project.

However, any citizen can challenge the city's acceptance of your EIR. Your project may be stopped while some citizen sues the city. If a court later decides that the city did not properly approve your EIR, you may have to re-do it. In this case it is the city's action that is being challenged directly. You are' involved because it is your EIR that the city approved.

The federal government and most states now have seizure and forfeiture laws by which the government can seize property and have it forfeited if the government suspects that the property was used for certain illegal purposes or was purchased with funds derived from those certain illegal purposes. The government uses these laws to combat racketeering and drug activity.

Under the seizure and forfeiture laws, your property can be seized by the government without a prior hearing. If, for example, a tenant uses your house for drug purposes, the house may be seized, and you may have to initiate a lawsuit to have it returned to you.

DISPUTE

There is no lawsuit if no dispute arises from the relationship. Disputes usually arise through disagreement, misrepresentation or the inability or unwillingness of a person to perform his or her duties.

Disagreements

Many disputes arise from disagreements. Disagreements can occur at the time the relationship begins or during its performance. Often clients who consult an attorney do not know what their duties are to the others in the relationship or what the others' duties are to them. If an agreement is not in writing or if the rules of the relationship are imposed by law, people often do not know what rules apply to them. Even where there is a written agreement, it is not uncommon to have a disagreement as to the obligations and duties imposed by certain terms.

Even when there is general agreement at the beginning of a relationship, disagreements may occur during the course of the relationship. This includes disagreements,

37

for example, involving the implementation of a business plan; injuries in personal injury cases; and rules of the road.

Misrepresentations

Honest disagreements do not always result in a lawsuit. However, a misrepresentation may be a reason for initiating a lawsuit. This is why it is important to have witnesses who can later testify in court as to the facts of a disputed situation.

In a contract situation, one party may have been induced to enter into the contract by misrepresenting the facts. The law recognizes two levels of misrepresentation, intentional and negligent. Intentional misrepresentation is also known as fraud. If you know what the facts are and represent them differently than you know them to be, then you have intentionally misrepresented the facts, or defrauded the other person. If you make some representation to the other person but you have no reasonable basis to believe that your representations are not true, then you are negligently misrepresenting the facts. In either case, when the true facts are later discovered, you may be sued.

Nonperformance

Any failure to perform duties in a relationship may result in a lawsuit. Nonperformance may occur in two ways. First, you may agree to buy a product and then not be able to pay for it. You are, therefore, unable to perform. This does not excuse your performance, and you may be sued. Second, you may be unwilling to perform. This occurs when you have agreed to buy a product and then change your mind. The effect is the same whether you are not able to perform or you do not want to perform. There may be instances in which you have a reason for not performing. For example, if the person you contracted with misrepresented the quality or type of the product, your performance may be excused. This is why lawsuits are complicated; when a person sues you for nonperformance, you could, in this example, counter-sue for misrepresentation.

DAMAGES

In nearly all cases, someone will have suffered an injury or damage before a lawsuit is filed. In the case of a lawsuit for fraud or negligence, some loss by the plaintiff is a requirement, an element of their cause of action. There are many ways to measure damages. In general, a party should be able to sue to collect all direct damages and consequential damages. Direct and consequential damages, when combined, are known as general damages or actual damages.

If, for example, you are in an accident, direct damages would include the cost to repair your car and your medical expenses, while consequential damages would include loss of income or the cost of having to rent a car while yours is being repaired. If you have a contract to sell goods, direct damages would include the loss of your expected profit from the sale, while consequential damages would include costs incurred to store the goods.

The only method that the courts have to award damages is to order the payment of money. All losses must be reduced to money. In a lawsuit involving a contract dispute or damage to property, damages are fairly easy to calculate. In cases involving personal injury, death or damage to some intangible right (such as civil rights), the task is more difficult.

Damages must be certain and measurable in most cases and not speculative. In a contract case or a case involving damage to property, the court will not speculate on the amount of damage. You will have to prove to the court the exact amount of your loss. In personal injury cases, damages are measured by medical bills, loss of earnings and other income due to the injury. In a case involving death, the courts will often look at the normal life expectancy and the earning capacity of the decedent to determine the amount of damages.

It may seem strange that some injuries are measured in money. For example, how much is it actually worth if a restaurant refuses to serve a person based on race, age or sexual preference? How much, beyond the cleanup cost, is it worth when somebody defaces a synagogue with anti-Semitic graffiti? As you can see, there may be no easy way to estimate monetary damage, but courts have determined that some rights are so important that the denial of those rights will allow a victim to recover substantial damages.

Even if a court finds that someone has invaded your rights, if it cannot find that you suffered any substantial loss or injury, the court may award nominal damages. Nominal damages are usually a trifling amount and can be awarded when the plaintiff has suffered an injury of some type but has failed to prove any specific amount of monetary damages.

It is also important to understand punitive, or exemplary, damages. There has been, over the years, much publicity concerning punitive damages. Punitive damages are different from other types of damages. They are not

41

based on the amount of loss suffered by the plaintiff; they are based on the amount of worth of the defendant. They are awarded not to compensate the plaintiff (although some plaintiffs certainly are rewarded with them quite well); they are awarded to punish, and make an example of, the defendant.

Punitive damages can be awarded if the judge or jury finds that the defendant acted with malice or wilfully to injure the plaintiff. Sometimes punitive damages can be awarded if the court finds that the defendant acted with callous disregard for the rights of the plaintiff. If someone acts intentionally to hurt another (such as by fraud), then punitive damages can be awarded. Punitive damages, however, will not be awarded in garden variety negligence cases (such as most traffic accidents).

A well plead punitive damages claim can sometimes settle a case rather quickly, since the plaintiff may not want to risk the possibility of suffering a punitive damages award. Generally, insurance companies are not allowed to pay for any punitive damages, so there will be no insurance coverage for these damages.

The public policy debate over punitive damages will probably continue to rage for the next several years. Special interest groups representing most business and industrial interests argue that punitive damages should be limited. They claim that punitive damages constitute an unearned windfall for some plaintiffs and not punitive damage awards are out of control. Special interest groups representing the consumer rights industry argue that punitive damages should be expanded as the only way to force big business to focus on producing products which are safer for the consumer. As usual, the issue is continually under debate.

EQUITABLE REMEDIES

In some cases, you do not have to show any loss or damages that you have suffered. You do, however, have to show that you are likely to suffer damage unless the defendant is stopped from doing something or is forced to do something. An injunction is a court order prohibiting somebody from doing something. An injunction can also require somebody to do something, but this type of injunction is very rare. If you have entered into an exclusive employment contract with a famous singer, the singer cannot sing for anybody else during your contract. If the singer threatens to work elsewhere for more money, you may not be able to prove how much that move will cost you, because the damages may be speculative. So you may try to obtain an injunction.

43

You could ask the court to issue an order forcing the singer to continue working for you, but since the Thirteenth Amendment to the United States Constitution abolished involuntary servitude, it is not very likely that a court will force the singer to work for you if he or she does not want to. On the other hand, you may well have a court issue an order prohibiting the singer from singing for another during the remaining term of the contract.

Another equitable remedy is specific performance. If you agree to sell your home, sign a contract and then change your mind, the buyer could ask the court to specifically enforce the contract. If the buyer is successful, the court could order you to sell your home at the agreed price and upon the agreed terms even if the value of the house has risen dramatically during the lawsuit.

If you are in a relationship - any relationship - in which a dispute occurs, you may be sued. The court may order you to do something, stop doing something or pay money. This should make it clear that litigation is not the most friendly way to handle problems but that the very purpose of litigation is to resolve these problems.

44

CHAPTER 3

THE LITIGATION PROCESS

How did you get into this lawsuit, anyway? Whether you are a defendant or the plaintiff, you may feel as if you have been swept away by the tide with no control over where you are going, and you are struggling to keep from drowning. Only by understanding the process that you have entered can you appreciate the different steps and understand what is likely to happen next. Proceeding through a lawsuit is full of surprises and uncertainty in any case, but knowing the process should limit the number of surprises. You can then present your case more effectively and be more helpful to your lawyer. Remember, it is your lawyers job to win for you. The more you can help, the easier that job will be for your lawyer.

We will follow two common types of lawsuits through the various stages of litigation. Probably the most common lawsuit is one that arises from a standard, garden-variety traffic accident. Even though your insurance company may pay for your representation in the lawsuit, you will still participate and assist in preparing your case. Under this example, assume you are the driver who made a left turn in front of an oncoming car. Both of you had a green light. The other car hit your car. Your car suffered damage, but you are generally uninjured except for some stiffness. The other car suffered somewhat less damage than yours, but the other driver suffered serious injuries. You are sued, so you are the defendant. The other driver sues you for the cost of repairing her car, for medical expenses and reconstructive surgery, for loss of earnings for the four months she cannot work and for future loss of earnings, since she is a model and now has scars on her face.

In the second example, assume you purchase a house directly from the owner. Three months after the purchase, you notice some significant damage to the house. There is significant cracking occurring in the walls and ceilings, and portions of the roof line appear to be sagging. You noticed none of this before you purchased the house. In questioning your neighbors, you discover that the house had some reinforcement work done to it two years earlier. The seller said nothing to you about the reinforcement work. You consult your local lawyer and file a lawsuit against both

46

the seller for not disclosing the preexisting problem and the company which performed the reinforcement work. In this lawsuit, you are the plaintiff. A construction expert hired by your lawyer says that it will cost about half of your purchase price to repair the house.

Both of these fact situations present interesting and sometimes difficult problems. Our purpose is not to discover who should win in either of these cases; our purpose is to examine the litigation system. We will examine how these two cases will be treated by the system. We will examine how much time it takes to go to trial and how much it may cost you. You will find out what your lawyer should be doing and what you will have to do to help with your case.

We will then proceed through the trial itself. Some trials worth several hundred thousand dollars but with simple facts may take only one day. Other trials can proceed for many days. The dollar amount is not a determining factor. The trial is an exciting and extremely dynamic process. We will examine how a trial is structured and learn what to expect from it.

Finally, we will review some alternative methods for resolving disputes. I do not expect alternative dispute resolution to replace litigation as the main arbiter of disputes, but it is becoming a more important part of the

47

litigation system. So, you are the defendant in the traffic accident case and the plaintiff in the real estate case. Let us proceed and see what we have to tackle and accomplish.

CHAPTER 4

THE NEED FOR A LAWYER

In both of these fact situations, you could have insurance which would provide an attorney to represent you. However, in both situations, we will ignore insurance so that you make all the decisions. Even if your insurance company represents you, you should still partake in the decision making process. The first decision to make is whether to contact a lawyer.

WHAT A LAWYER CAN CONTRIBUTE

In the traffic accident case, you have been sued, and the question is what to do next. In the real estate case, you have just noticed the damage to your house, and you need

49

to evaluate your alternatives. In both cases, a lawyer can provide objective analysis. Lawyers are trained to look at facts and apply the appropriate law to those facts to predict the likely outcomes.

Your lawyer will have a business relationship with you. Do not expect your lawyer to become personally involved in your problem. That is not to say that lawyers are insensitive to their clients problems. Proceeding with a lawsuit can be emotionally difficult and a lawyer should be sensitive to the difficulties when recommending alternative ways to proceed in the lawsuit.

In addition to providing an objective analysis a lawyer can contribute his or her drafting skills. Good lawyers can write several variations of a letter to make the message clear and establish the legal consequences.

It is fairly common to consult a lawyer and then not hire that lawyer. Especially in the field of family law, people often want to handle their own divorces, but will occasionally consult an attorney to make sure they understand the consequences of their actions. Many times, someone will implement the lawyer's advice and resolve the dispute. Whether you hire a lawyer or whether you follow a lawyer's advice is your choice. If, however, you hire a lawyer to represent you in your lawsuit, be prepared to have your lawyer handle the lawsuit and retain control of all aspects of the case.

This is not to say that a lawyer does not need to keep you informed about the progress of the case and consult you on all major decisions, therefore, allowing you to retain control over significant decisions such as settlement decisions. For economic reasons, you may also wish to delay a particularly expensive undertaking, such as taking a deposition. But your lawyer knows the procedures and the rules of evidence and may disagree with your decisions. Although you should follow your lawyer's advice, you have the final say on all matters. If you and your lawyer disagree on many issues, he or she may want to withdraw from the case and you may want to find another lawyer.

A case is decided based on many pieces of information. You may concentrate on one or a few pieces of information that you may consider crucial to your case. Your lawyer, on the other hand, will know that some of these pieces of information may not, for example, be admissible as evidence, and if they are, they may not have the importance to the outcome of the case which you have attributed to them. A lawyer is skilled at weaving a tapestry of these pieces of information so that the final

51

product results in a strong case which hopefully you can win. However, a lawyer cannot choose the pieces of information. He or she must work with what is available to him or her and then choose the best pieces of information which are available and have value as evidence.

Although most judges try to accommodate those who choose to represent themselves, they do so only to be fair to one who they perceive is at a disadvantage by not having a lawyer represent him or her. This is not necessarily a fair perception, but it is a common one. Most individuals who represent themselves, in pro per, are very strong with the substantive issues but are at a distinct disadvantage in matters of evidence and procedure. One is usually not as effective arguing only substantive issues unless there is also an effective use of the rules of evidence and procedure.

Finally, a lawyer can contribute advocacy skills, the ability to argue effectively. A lawyer's argument includes a controlled, rational, logical argument of legal issues. A lawyer can present the facts that were produced at trial and argue their significance to the judge or jury in a logical, concise manner.

ECONOMIC CONSIDERATIONS

A very significant factor in deciding whether to hire a lawyer is the fee that you will pay. There are basically three different types of fee arrangements. In addition to legal fees, you will be expected to pay any out-of-pocket expenses incurred by your lawyer. The key to understanding out-of-pocket expenses is understanding what you will be charged for and in what amounts. Ask if you will be charged for telephone charges, photocopying costs, mileage, the costs of a court reporter or the costs for normal services such as messengers, postage and process servers. Some lawyers also charge for items such as computer time. All of these costs are over and above the legal fees.

For example, it is difficult to motivate a lawyer to vigorously pursue a contingency fee case, if it appears that the outcome will be minimal. Likewise, when a lawyer in a firm is constantly reminded to bill a certain number of hours each month, he or she can be inclined to spend his or her time on the matters on which it will be easiest to bill the most time. I believe most lawyers act quite ethically when in their billing practices, but you should be aware of the subtle pressures that both you and your lawyer will have based upon the type of legal fee arrangement you decide to use for your case.

Set or Fixed Fee Arrangement

It is uncommon to use a set or fixed fee arrangement in litigation. It is more appropriate in certain standardized transactions, such as, creating a corporation or writing a will or trust. On occasion, though, a lawyer may agree to handle a lawsuit for a set or fixed amount of money. It is not wise to request this type of fee arrangement unless your case is very simple. The benefit of a set or fixed fee is that the client knows exactly how much the lawyer will charge for his or her work. The disadvantage is that, if the case is easier than anticipated, the client may feel cheated for paying so much for so little work. Likewise, if the case becomes more complex than anticipated when the fee is set or fixed, a lawyer may feel that he or she is not being properly compensated, and he or she could lose interest in the case.

54

Contingency Fee Arrangement

A contingency fee is the most common fee arrangement for the plaintiff in, for example, our traffic accident case. In a contingency fee arrangement, the lawyer receives, as a fee, a percentage of the judgement. If the plaintiff loses, the lawyer will not receive a fee. Since the lawyer is taking a chance on not receiving a fee, there are two primary rules for contingency fees. First, liability of the other party must be fairly certain and easy to prove at trial. For example, in our traffic accident case, you are probably the one at fault, since you turned left in front of oncoming traffic. If you are sued, this rule is easy to satisfy, because it is fairly certain that you will be found at fault. On the other hand, if you were to sue the other driver and ask your attorney to work on a contingency fee basis, it is unlikely that the first rule would be satisfied since it is not clear that the other driver was at fault.

The other rule is that there must be a fund of money from which to collect a judgment or settlement. This is where insurance becomes important. Insurance companies usually have the money to pay a judgement or settlement. If you receive a judgment against an insured, insurance companies will usually pay the judgment. In many states, insurance companies have a duty to settle cases if at all possible. Therefore, if it is likely that the other driver is at fault and the other driver has insurance, your case is a good one for a contingency fee. If either of those conditions do not apply, many lawyers will not take your case on a contingency fee.

Many lawyers have turned down cases where the client was badly injured and the other driver was clearly at fault, but there was no insurance. You can receive all the judgments possible, but unless there is some fund or property from which to receive payment, the judgments are worthless. You may want to pursue your case on principle, but your lawyer needs to make a business decision whether to spend the time and effort necessary to win a case for which he or she is unlikely to be paid.

Contingency fees do not lend themselves, for example, to our real estate lawsuit or, for that matter, to nearly any type of business litigation. In business litigation, it is frequently unclear at the beginning who is at fault. Business cases also allege intentional acts for which there is no insurance. Now, if you are suing a large corporation and your lawyer knows legally that the corporation is at fault, your lawyer may consider a contingency fee if the damages are large enough, but that type of case is rare. Business cases take many twists and turns before they proceed to trial and generally involve more complex issues than traffic accident or personal injury cases. From a

56

business perspective, it does not make sense for a lawyer to handle a case if the expected fee is far lower than the reasonable time and effort expended to proceed with the case to trial.

If a lawyer takes a case on a contingency fee basis, his or her job is to settle the case quickly. The more time the lawyer spends, the less money the lawyer will receive as a fee. With rare exceptions, the contingency fee lawyer considers that he or she is losing money by proceeding to trial. The money from the settlement of an accident case, for example, usually is divided three ways. First, the physicians who treated the other driver's injuries and the mechanics who repaired the car are paid, then the lawyer takes his or her fee and the winner of the lawsuit receives the balance.

If the case does not have a large settlement value, or if the bills are higher than expected, there may not be any money remaining for the winner of the lawsuit. Sometimes, even a lawyer will not receive his or her whole fee. Most lawyers who represent plaintiff's in contingency fee cases are very good at obtaining settlements to ensure the payment and receipt of his or her fee.

Hourly Fee

The most common arrangement for legal fees in the real estate case and in most business cases is for an attorney to bill on an hourly basis.

Under this method of billing a lawyer bills for each hour he or she spends on your case. The total dollar amount of your legal fees is a function of how much time your lawyer spends on your case. Since there are at least two sides to every lawsuit, you must appreciate that your lawyer does not have complete control over how much time must be spent on the case. Even if your lawyer wants to spend a minimum amount of time on your case in order to keep fees low, the other side may deluge your lawyer with discovery and motions with which your lawyer must respond in a timely fashion so as to not jeopardize your lawsuit. Every time your lawyer must respond to the opposing lawyer, it costs you money.

Most lawyers have a particular billing rate. Billing rates vary widely in different parts of the country. In some parts of the country, lawyers will bill between $80.00 - to - $100.00 per hour. In other parts of the country, legal fees average $200.00 - to - $300.00 per hour. Law is an industry

58

that is subject to its own market conditions. Legal fees go up and, occasionally, down based on those market conditions. Do not expect the market conditions that affect legal fees to follow the general economy. A down economy often results in increases in litigation and a greater need for trial attorneys.

All lawyers who bill by the hour divide the hour into fractions, usually from one-tenth to one-quarter of an hour. Those divisions are the minimum time unit that the lawyer will bill for any activity. For example, assume your lawyer bills at a rate of $150.00 per hour. If he or she has a three minute telephone call on your case, you will be charged $15.00, if his or her minimum time unit is one-tenth of an hour, but you will be charged $37.50, if his minimum time unit is one-quarter of an hour. An eight minute telephone call will not cost you more if your lawyer's minimum time unit is one-quarter of an hour, because eight minutes is still within the first quarter hour. That eight minute call, however, will cost you $30 if your lawyer's minimum time unit is one-tenth of an hour, because eight minutes is beyond the first tenth of an hour, which is equal to six minutes.

You should also be aware of how many time units will be charged for certain specified activities. For example, some firms will charge a minimum of two-tenths of an hour for telephone calls or three-tenths of an hour for letters either sent or received. Some lawyers will charge you for a minimum half day in court even if you only spend a couple hours in court that day. Aside from minimum charges for certain activities, you should know what activities will result in charges. Will you be charged for telephone calls, for travel time, for secretary's or paralegal's time (and at what rate will you be charged)? Will you be charged for time that your lawyer spends consulting with other lawyers in his firm?

The benefit of paying for legal services by the hour is that the client pays only for the time expended. Whereas a contingency fee accrues to the lawyer's benefit if the case settles quickly, an hourly fee accrues to the client's benefit if the case settles quickly. The problem with hourly fees is that the legal fees can exceed the amount in controversy. At your first meeting with your lawyer, you should insist on his or her best estimate of the total amount of legal fees you will need to spend on your case. As mentioned above, he or she will not be able to assure you of the total legal fees, but he or she should be able to tell you the likely range of fees. During your case, you should keep legal fees in mind in considering what actions to pursue. More than any other type of billing system, hourly fees are important when considering settlement proposals, because, until the case is over, the fees will continue to accrue and you will be required to pay them.

Hourly fees, more than other types of fee arrangements, demand that you know whether you are likely to be able to recover legal fees if you win your case. In the United States the usual rule is that each party pays his or her own legal fees unless: (1) there is a contract which is the subject matter of the lawsuit; and (2) the contract provides for the winner to recover legal fees; or (3) a statute provides for the payment of legal fees by the loser.

The general rule is riddled with exceptions so it is important to ask your lawyer about the likelihood of recovering legal fees if you should win your case. Remember that recovery of fees is a two-edged sword; if you win, you will recover attorneys fees, but if you lose, you will pay the winner's attorneys fees.

All of the foregoing are considered legitimate methods for charging fees by most lawyers, but you are entitled to know at the beginning of your relationship with your lawyer what fee system he or she will use in connection with your case. Your lawyer may not be able to predict what the total fees will be with great accuracy, but you should be able to understand what you are going to be paying for in your lawsuit. Many clients are intimidated by lawyers and are afraid of asking about fees and costs. On the other hand, many lawyers do not discuss fees with clients. Most lawyers do what they do because they want to practice law, not because they are good business people.

Also, I believe, some lawyers are embarrassed by the amount that they charge.

The most important item to consider at the beginning of your relationship with your lawyer, next to the objective, legal analysis of your problem, is to establish a complete understanding of the fee structure. Legal fees are one of the largest problem areas between lawyers and their clients.

It is important to remember that a lawyer does not usually provide a product that you can see and touch. A large percentage of the work performed by a lawyer is done out of your sight. Neither you nor your lawyer can maintain the trust and confidence in each other that is necessary to successfully conduct a trial if there are concerns pertaining to billing. Whatever the fee arrangement, you should demand a written fee agreement.

CHAPTER 5

THE TIME IT TAKES TO GO TO TRIAL

Why does it take so long to go to trial? Most states have statutes that require that a trial be started within a certain time after a complaint is filed with the court. This helps to prevent cases from remaining dormant for many years. Some states require that trials start within one year after the complaint is filed with the court. In others, a lawsuit can continue for five years before the trial must start. We will discuss these time limits and court congestion further in Chapter 8.

For our purposes, we will divide a lawsuit into three different time categories. First, is the time from the filing of the lawsuit to a time about thirty to sixty days before trial. This time, and all of the activities that take place within it, will be reviewed in this chapter. The second time category, lasting for thirty to sixty days before trial, is known as trial preparation and is covered in Chapter 7. The final time category is the trial itself which is covered in Chapter 8.

You may wonder why only the last thirty to sixty days before trial is known as trial preparation. This first time category involves trial preparation but the focus is on the time it takes to establish the issues and gather factual information. This time can last from several months to a few years. Many different things can occur during this time period. As a general rule the activity on a lawsuit is high at the very beginning when the pleadings are prepared, initial investigation is completed and any pleading motions are filed. After the initial pleading stage is completed, the activity in most cases settles down so that there is little or no activity for several months.

Those times of low activity are punctuated with occasional outbursts of discovery. Discovery is a formal process and can be very expensive and time-consuming. Discovery activity usually shows up as peaks in the generally low-activity stage. Then, as the lawsuit enters the trial preparation stage, the activity reaches its highest levels and, depending on the nature of the case, can be sustained at that high level through the entire trial preparation and trial stages. Remember that the activity level translates directly into legal fees, if your lawyer bills by the hour.

PLEADINGS

The purpose of pleadings is to: (1) explain to the defendants why they are being sued; and (2) explain to the plaintiff what defenses the defendants may use in their case. All lawsuits start with the filing of a complaint or a claim. In the complaint, the plaintiff will allege what the plaintiff believes the defendants did to cause damage or injury to the plaintiff. In our real estate case, you are the plaintiff, so you would file the complaint and pay a filing fee with the clerk of the court. In your complaint, you must name everyone who you claim has some liability to you arising from your purchase of the allegedly defective house. Remember, the information in the complaint is not evidence. What you claim is merely an allegation. You later will have to provide evidence to support your allegations.

Your lawyer will take the information you give him or her and after an initial investigation will conduct legal research to determine the causes of action which can be maintained based on the available information. In your case, you may have causes of action for negligent misrepresentation against both the sellers and the real estate brokers (both yours and the sellers'), for fraud against the sellers and, possibly, against the real estate brokers, for breach of contract against the sellers, for breach of fiduciary duty against your real estate agent, for breach of warranty against the construction company and for improper or defective construction against the construction company. Not all of these causes of action are available in all states, but you start to realize that a considerable amount of work is invested in the preparation of a complaint.

Remember, most lawyers want to keep cases as simple as possible, but your lawyer would rather include some questionable causes of action that can be removed later than not include them and later be sued for malpractice because, by the time the case goes to trial, one of them would have been the most effective claim in the lawsuit and it is too late to include it in the complaint. If you decide that you do not want to pursue a particular cause of action or a particular defendant, your lawyer should carefully explain the ramifications of that decision.

After the complaint is prepared and filed, it must be personally served on the defendants. In most cases, this is not a difficult process. Interestingly, though, if you have a defendant that is living in another state, or if you do not know where that defendant lives or works, or the defendant is aware that you are trying to serve process on him or her and actively tries to avoid the process server, this process may take some time. Occasionally, a defendant seems to have disappeared. In those cases, you must make a good faith effort to find the defendant, usually by hiring a private investigator. If the defendant cannot be found through a diligent search, the court will usually allow you to serve that defendant by publication. After the court issues you an order allowing you to serve by publication, then the publication notice may be filed in the proper newspapers. Once a specified time after publication has lapsed, the defendant is served.

Once a defendant is served, the defendant has a certain time within which to file responsive pleadings. The defendant can file an answer to a complaint admitting certain allegations and denying other allegations. The defendant also can file and serve a pleading motion of some type. A pleading motion is one that challenges the pleading. Although they may be found under different names in different states, there are two primary kinds of pleading motions, a demurrer and a motion to strike.

Demurrers challenge the very nature of the complaint. Basically, a demurrer says, "even if all of the allegations against me alleged in the complaint are true, I

67

still do not have any liability to the plaintiff". For example, in your real estate case, the construction company may file a demurrer to your cause of action that alleges a breach of warranty. Breach of warranty is a cause of action based on some contract relationship, and the construction company may claim that they never had any contract with you, so you cannot win under any circumstances against them on that cause of action. Demurrers can be directed to the entire complaint or to any single cause of action.

Motions to strike are not the same as demurrers, although they are often confused. A motion to strike can be directed to the entire complaint, a single cause of action, a single sentence or even a single word. If a part of the complaint is improper or a sham, a motion to strike that part of the complaint may be filed. For example, if your complaint against the construction company requested punitive damages, and your state does not authorize punitive damages for the causes of action you have against the construction company, the construction company will most likely file a motion to strike that part of your complaint requesting punitive damages against them.

If a pleading motion is filed, a hearing will be scheduled in court. You will have a certain amount of time to research, prepare and file a document stating your opposition to the demurrer or the motion to strike. The court at the hearing may or may not listen to oral arguments. If the defendant loses the motion, he or she will have a certain time within which to file an answer. If you lose, you may be given a certain amount of time to amend your complaint. It is possible to have to amend a complaint three or four times before the court either requires that you file no more amendments or requires the defendant to answer the complaint. Even then the pleading stage is not completed, since defendants will often file cross-complaints or cross-claims.

When a defendant files a cross-complaint, he or she can name the plaintiff or any other defendants as cross-defendants. He or she can also name other people who are not yet involved in the lawsuit. In this way, the case can become much larger than the plaintiff originally anticipated and can cause an increase in legal fees. New parties brought into the case, of course, must be personally served, and they are entitled to file their own pleading motions. Depending upon the number of new parties, the diligence and efficiency used in filing their pleadings, and the actual time required to hear the pleading motions, the pleading stage can take a considerable amount of time.

INVESTIGATION

You may expect that the investigation stage should be completed before a complaint is prepared, and that the plaintiff's lawyer should conduct preliminary investigation before filing a complaint. Usually, it is not practical to conduct all possible investigation before a complaint must be filed. In addition, a defendant does not have the luxury of knowing when a complaint will be filed. A defendant is already under certain time pressures when he or she first learns of the lawsuit, so there is little time for the defendant to investigate before filing an answer to the complaint, which usually must be filed within thirty days.

In your traffic accident case, this investigation includes talking to any witnesses to the accident and obtaining a copy of the police report. Information that you obtain through your own investigation may not be admissible evidence. A certified copy of a public record - like a police report - may be admissible as evidence, but what a witness tells you is not admissible unless the witness testifies in court.

Since discovery is available to all participants in the lawsuit, you or your lawyer will make tactical decisions whether to use informal investigation or whether to formalize your witnesses' testimony through discovery. Investigation also includes consulting with experts. In your traffic accident case, an accident reconstruction specialist could be consulted. In your real estate case, your investigation could include consulting with geologists or structural engineers.

The purpose of investigation is to find out how much evidence you have, or how strong your evidence is, to support your case. An investigation should rely only upon those who agree with your position or with neutral parties. Those who are opposed to your position, and third parties who cannot voluntarily disclose information, will not cooperate with your informal investigation. For those individuals, you must use formal discovery procedures.

DISCOVERY

Discovery is used to gather and preserve information that supports your position. You can, for example, take the deposition of a witness who supports your position. Normally, you would not do that unless you are concerned that the witness will not be available at the time of trial or unless the witness is weak in his or her recollection, and you want to record the story which is most favorable to your position. Generally, discovery is used to discover the other side's evidence.

Formal discovery takes different forms and has very different rules in different states. Typically, discovery has four basic forms. First, you can send another party written questions known as interrogatories. If the interrogatories are proper under local requirements, then the person to whom they are directed must answer them, under oath, in writing. In many places, there is no limit on the number of interrogatories that you can send to any other participant, and you do not have to send all of your interrogatories all at one time. Because of perceived abuses of this system, some states now limit the number of interrogatories that you can send to other participants or that they can send to you. Interrogatories are useful, because they give responding parties time to research information necessary to answer the questions, so it is difficult for responding parties to answer "I do not remember."

The second type of formal discovery is the oral deposition. In a deposition, the lawyer for the person requesting the deposition asks questions of another participant in the lawsuit or of a witness. The deposition is conducted face to face. All parties to the lawsuit and their lawyers are entitled to be at the deposition and ask questions. The questions and answers will be recorded by a court reporter. The deposition also may be videotaped. The benefits of depositions are numerous. Primarily, they provide an opportunity to see how the person will appear as a witness and how the person conducts himself or herself under cross-examination. Since the witness is testifying without having the testimony filtered through a lawyer (as is done with all written forms of discovery), you are likely to obtain candid answers.

In a deposition, you are more likely to hear that the witness does not remember certain things. Certainly some witnesses have very selective memories, but many witnesses do not remember things simply because they are answering questions without researching whatever backup information they may have. When you have your deposition taken, your job is not to place all of your story out in the open. It is your job only to answer the specific questions asked of you. The most common mistake people make in testifying at a deposition is to disclose too much information. Subject to certain exceptions, if the person asking the questions does not ask you for a crucial bit of information, you do not provide that information. Depositions also provide an opportunity for your attorney to see the other attorney in action and assess his or her questioning abilities.

A deposition may also be the best method for obtaining information from an independent witness, such as a bank, a doctor or an escrow holder, who cannot divulge

73

the information voluntarily, without direction from a court order. Depending upon the nature of the case and the number of witnesses, there could be several depositions, which could last for quite some time. Depositions may last for only a few hours, if deposing a witness, to several days if deposing a party to the lawsuit.

Requests for admissions are another form of written discovery by which you ask one of the other participants in the lawsuit to admit certain facts. The person to whom they are directed has a certain amount of time to respond in writing either admitting or denying the particular facts. There is often some mechanism (sometimes through the use of interrogatories) in which you can require an explanation as to a person's failure to admit facts that were not admitted in the pleadings. There is also usually some mechanism for having the facts deemed admitted, if the person to whom the requests are directed does not respond to them in a timely manner.

The last main category of formal discovery is a request for inspection of documents or other items. A party sends a request to another person involved in the lawsuit directing that person to produce certain documents or other items at a specified time and place for inspection and copying, if applicable. The person then must provide the original documents or other items for inspection unless you have indicated that copies would be sufficient. This

74

method of discovery is particularly helpful if there is a question as to whether a document has been changed or if it is necessary to determine the exact terms of certain documents.

Through discovery, a party looks for the strengths and weaknesses of the other side's case. Discovery can be quite time-consuming. If a party does not respond to discovery or does not fully answer the questions, then a motion can be made to the court to order further or more complete responses. Some courts will readily fine or jail a party who does not fully comply with discovery requests. Any motion to order further responses is made in writing. The witness has the right to file opposition to the motion. At the hearing, if the court orders further responses, the witness will be given a certain amount of time to provide the further responses.

Each participant in a case will be conducting discovery. If you are a major player in the case, you or your lawyer may want to attend every deposition, review every response to interrogatories or requests for admission and review each document produced. If there are many participants in the lawsuit, discovery can become a very burdensome process. It is, in varying degrees, encouraged by all states and the federal government as a way to prevent surprises at trial. If a party does not request sufficient information through the discovery process, then its admissability may be limited at trial. If, however, a party requested the information but did not receive it, it may not be admissible at the trial.

SUMMARY JUDGMENTS

After some or all discovery is completed, a party may bring a motion for a summary judgment. A summary judgment motions says that, based upon the facts that are not in dispute, the person making the motion should win as a matter of law. If a summary judgment motion is successful, then that person wins his part of the case without having to go through the trial. Because the results of a summary judgment motion can be so dramatic, they are defended vigorously. Because courts are oriented toward granting each individual his day in court, many judges do not grant summary judgment motions.

A ruling in a summary judgment motion determines whether there are any issues of fact that need to be decided. If the facts that have been established through discovery demonstrate that the participants do not disagree on the most important facts, then the judge can apply the appropriate rules of law to the facts and decide who wins. If there are no important facts to be decided, then there is no need for a trial. Remember, a jury or the judge at trial, is a fact finder. They hear conflicting testimony and decide which facts are true and are supported by the evidence. If there are no major facts in dispute, the trial becomes unnecessary.

The summary judgment motion has a related motion that is usually made at the same time. This is the motion for summary adjudication of issues. In it, the person who brings the motion claims that, even if there are some issues of fact yet to be decided, some issues are not disputed. If the court agrees, it will declare some facts not to be disputed. Even though the trial will continue, the undisputed facts will not have to be proven at the trial, so no evidence need be presented on those issues. Obviously, this motion has great potential for limiting the issues to be decided at the trial and shortening the trial.

OTHER APPEARANCES

Each state has its own requirements for other appearances in court during this stage of the lawsuit. Often courts within a state will have different requirements. You or your lawyer may have to appear in court any number of times for status conferences, trial setting conferences,

77

general trial conferences or mandatory settlement conferences. We will not spend much time on these, since they vary so much from state to state. However, mention must be made of mandatory settlement conferences. Some courts have established a system whereby certain judges are identified to settle cases. In several states, at least one court will set aside one week each quarter when all civil courtrooms, jury rooms, hallways and closets are put to use handling settlement conferences. Although the court's purposes are not particularly altruistic, it may spend a considerable time trying to convince you that you should settle your case. You are under no duty to settle; but you may be under tremendous pressure from the court, and possibly from your own lawyer, to settle the case.

REEVALUATION

During each stage of a lawsuit, it is important to continue to reevaluate your case. It is particularly important in the investigation and discovery processes, since these stages continue to produce new and different information. Some of that information will support your case; some of it will not. You will remain emotionally involved in your case, but your perspective will change depending on whether it is progressing well at the time.

If your lawyer places pressure on you to settle your case, do not mistake that for not supporting your position. Many lawyers work hard at trying to settle cases simply because they know that there are many variables in a trial. Especially if you and your opponent disagree on basic facts of the case, you should remember that the judge or jury will decide which facts are supported by the evidence. The decision is not based on who is right or wrong. Remember that the judge or jury has no more reason to believe you than it has to believe your opponent.

As the case progresses toward trial, the issues that need to be decided at trial will become narrower and more refined. That is the main purpose of this stage of a lawsuit. Through discovery and motions, the issues that are actually in dispute become more clearly defined so that they can be presented at the trial in a meaningful and concise manner. As the issues narrow and you begin to focus on the remaining significant issues, you may view your case differently than you did earlier, especially if you leave your mind open to all the new information that has developed through discovery or your own investigation.

The lawsuit is not a goal in and of itself; it is, rather, the process to reach a conclusion. If you remember that the lawsuit is only the means to an end, you can continue to reevaluate the end and make settlement decisions accordingly.

If, on the other hand, you become wedded to the process rather than to the end to be accomplished, you may lose sight of your desired result or not recognize when your desired result may no longer be realistic. I am not suggesting that you spend every night of a lawsuit agonizing over whether you have been doing the right thing. Rather, you should remain open to new information as it becomes available and realistically reevaluate your position, from time to time, based on the best information available.

CHAPTER 6

THE COST OF LITIGATION

There are many costs of litigation. Some people argue that litigation takes a toll on our society. Certainly. it costs money to maintain the court systems that we all pay for with our taxes. Litigation may also exact a toll in broken relationships, emotional strain and lost income. This chapter, however, examines the direct cost to you of your lawsuit.

JUDGMENT OR SETTLEMENT

If you are a defendant or a cross-defendant, you stand the risk of suffering a judgment against you that you will have to pay. If you are the plaintiff, and not also a

81

cross-defendant, you would not have to suffer any money loss if you lose your lawsuit, unless you are required to pay the winner's attorneys fees. Any settlement payment, obviously, is somewhat less onerous because you agree to make it. That is not to say that you want to make it. Lawyers define a good settlement as one in which no one is happy with the result.

Typically, people are not happy with their settlements, but they agree to make them in order to terminate the lawsuit and avoid the uncertainty of a trial. Do not think that you are safe from making settlement payments just because you are the plaintiff. I have seen cases where the only person who pays any money in settlement of a case is the plaintiff. As strange as it seems, as a case twists and turns its way toward trial, it sometimes makes sense for the plaintiff to make a settlement payment.

COSTS

We discussed costs in Chapter 4. In addition to the office and travel costs incurred by your lawyer, there are a number of other costs involved in a lawsuit. To file a lawsuit, you must pay a filing fee. A defendant also pays an appearance fee when he first appears in the case. Usually a defendant first appears when he files his answer. Every motion that is filed is accompanied by a motion fee. Then there are the costs for specialty services: the copying service that copies records that you have subpoenaed; the court reporter who transcribes deposition testimony; the video operator who tapes a deposition; or the investigator who locates your defendants or your witnesses. Depositions, especially, can be quite expensive. In addition to legal fees, the court reporter can charge you several hundred dollars for the transcript of a deposition.

In most states, any witness who is not a participant in the lawsuit is entitled to a witness fee, regardless of whether you call that witness to a deposition or to the trial. If you call an expert witness, you will have to pay that expert his or her fee for taking the time to prepare for trial and to appear as a witness.

Occasionally, you will also pay a witness who is not an expert witness. You can force any person to appear as a witness at a deposition or at the trial, but if you want him to be a friendly or cooperative witness, sometimes you will consider paying him the amount he would lose in pay by appearing in the deposition or the trial.

If you have a jury, you may also have to pay jury fees day by day as the trial progresses. Depending on the complexity of the case, the number of expert witnesses, the number of depositions and the amount of time it will take to prepare for the trial and to conduct the trial, the costs of a lawsuit can be quite expensive.

LEGAL FEES

As mentioned in Chapter 4, if you are the plaintiff in a personal injury case, you probably have a contingency fee arrangement with your lawyer. You will not pay any legal fees while the case is in progress. All legal fees will be deducted from your ultimate winnings or settlement. In the very simplest of cases, such as simple evictions and bankruptcies, you may be able to pay a set fee for the entire matter. Everyone else, including defendants in personal injury cases, are probably paying hourly legal fees.

Since billing rates vary so widely around the country, it is difficult to determine exactly how many dollars your lawsuit will cost, so I will present legal fees to you as a function of time. The time spent on a particular type of case is the same regardless of the lawyer's billing rate.[3] Business litigation can include real estate litigation.

---

[3]The following analysis was published by James Wawro, "The Price Tag of Business Litigation," Los Angeles Lawyer, June 1979.

Business litigation can be divided into categories for simple, intermediate and complex cases. In all cases both the lawyer and the client have to expend substantial amounts of time on the case. This analysis assumes that the case is not a routine case, such as simple divorce, simple bankruptcy or simple eviction. Those cases can often be handled for fewer hours. There are many lawyers who specialize in just those types of cases.

You can expect that the time spent would be greater on a complex case than on an intermediate case and greater on an intermediate case than on a simple case. For this purpose, we will divide your lawsuit into six different time elements:

1. Analysis and preliminaries (Chapter 4).
2. Pleadings and pleading motions (Chapter 5).
3. Discovery (Chapter 5).
4. Discovery motions and other motions (Chapter 5).
5. Trial Preparation (Chapter 7).
6. Trial (Chapter 8).

At the top of the next page is a table of the number of hours that you could expect your lawyer to spend on the different types of business lawsuits.

Time Element and Type of Case

	Simple	Intermediate	Complex
1.	20 hrs	50 hrs	105 hrs
2.	5 hrs	15 hrs	200 hrs
3.	100 hrs	195 hrs	390 hrs
4.	30 hrs	150 hrs	400 hrs
5.	39 hrs	195 hrs	445 hrs
6.	30 hrs	60 hrs	108 hrs
	224 hrs	665 hrs	1,648 hrs

The vast majority of cases in which you would become involved will fall in the simple category, but it does not take too much imagination to forecast the time involved in an intermediate or a complex lawsuit. If a lawsuit involves business secrets or environmental cleanup or securities problems, it easily could become complex. These categories do not consider the most difficult types of cases, such as anti-trust or asbestos cases. Those cases easily reach beyond the scope of these categories.

An often overlooked cost in litigation is the time the client spends on the case. The client must be involved because there are certain items which are handled more efficiently by the client than by the attorney. At the top of the next page is a table setting forth the time you could expect to spend on these types of cases.

Time Element and Type of Case

	Simple	Intermediate	Complex
1.	6 hrs	20 hrs	40 hrs
2.	3 hrs	10 hrs	50 hrs
3.	31 hrs	114 hrs	312 hrs
4.	7 hrs	20 hrs	50 hrs
5.	17 hrs	60 hrs	134 hrs
6.	30 hrs	60 hrs	108 hrs
	94 hrs	284 hrs	694 hrs

The person who developed this analysis bases these figures on a number of assumptions regarding how much time it takes to complete certain tasks; how many items need to be completed; and how frequently the client is needed to complete these tasks. He also assumes that there will not be undue harassment by either side and that the case will proceed to trial. All lawyers know that 90% to 95% of all cases do not proceed to trial, but they must prepare them as if they will go to trial. Your lawyer may handle your case somewhat differently, and that may either

87

increase or decrease the time necessary to properly handle the case. The point is, however, that a lawsuit is an expensive proposition.

The information in this chapter is another reason that your lawyer may try to convince you of the merits of settling your case. Only when you can compare the cost to you of settling your case to the cost of continuing with it will you be able to make an informed decision regarding settlement.

CHAPTER 7

PREPARING FOR TRIAL

The last thirty to sixty days before the trial date is when you and your lawyer must prepare for trial. All that has been completed previously has been directed at gathering information and narrowing the issues which will be decided at the trial. At this stage, the client and lawyer focus on the relevant information and organize it for trial. Now is also the time to prepare all of the evidence that you want presented on your behalf at the trial. Finally, this is when you prepare your legal arguments in a concise and convincing form.

There have been many books written on what to do during the last sixty days before trial. Your lawyer probably has one of them. Those books discuss in detail the many steps that must be completed before the start of the trial and several techniques for completing each of those steps. There are many different approaches on how to complete these steps.

The purpose of this book is not to teach you how to complete these steps. That would involve an exhaustive study of the steps and the different theories on how they should be handled. Instead, We will discuss the main steps, what is involved in each step, and why each step is important. Through this process you will see why so much activity takes place, and why so many cases settle, right before trial.

EVIDENCE

Your investigation has given you all the pieces of information available to support you claims. In formal discovery, you have converted some of the information gathered in your investigation into evidence, or you have discovered what pieces of information the other side has to support its claims. All of those pieces of information can be analogized to puzzle pieces that have been placed in a pile for later reference.

As each puzzle piece has been gathered, the general picture has become clearer in your mind. Only those who have proceeded through the information-gathering process have an idea as to the whole picture. All others, such as those who have read about your case in the newspapers, have no clear picture of your case, since their view of the final picture is based on very few pieces of the puzzle.

During the information-gathering stage, your lawyer may have put the border of the puzzle together, but most of the pieces have been left in the pile for later use. Now is the time to complete the puzzle. Your case must be presented to a judge or jury who knows little or nothing about the facts of your case. We will assume for the moment that your case will be presented to a jury. The jury's decision will be based on the parts of the puzzle that are presented to them. It is the role of your lawyer to present as clear a picture as possible of all of the facts of your case.

In all likelihood, your information-gathering has not uncovered every single piece of the puzzle. In addition, the rules of evidence will not allow all of the information to be presented at the trial. For any number of reasons, some pieces of information are considered unreliable or not relevant to the issues in your lawsuit. So the jury will not see all pieces of the puzzle. Now, some parts of the puzzle tend to support your claims, and other parts of the puzzle

91

tend to support the claims of the other side. There may be other parts of the puzzle that tend to indicate that neither side should win.

Your lawyer will organize all of the pieces of information so that the entire puzzle, or as much of it as possible, is completed. He or she must have as much of the entire puzzle completed as possible, so he or she will not be surprised at the trial when certain unpleasant pieces of information are presented. In every case, some unpleasant pieces of information (that you wish did not exist) will be presented at the trial. Even though the complete puzzle exists, your lawyer will not present all of it to the jury.

Of course, the pieces that are irrelevant or unreliable will not be shown to the jury. Then each side will present those pieces of the puzzle that most support its own position. If one side is better at presenting all of its pieces of the puzzle to the jury, or if one side has a clearer picture of its part of the puzzle, the jury will see a more complete picture supporting that side.

How are these puzzle pieces or pieces of information presented to the jury? They are presented in the form of evidence which exists in two basic forms: oral testimony and written documents. You already know what information your witnesses have available to them. Your witnesses, however, cannot just stand up in front of the jury and tell them your story. Evidence is presented by the witnesses by having the witnesses answer questions. The witnesses are not supposed to present evidence which is not responsive to a question. So your lawyer must prepare the questions that are needed to elicit all of the information necessary to prove your claims.

Your lawyer then reviews those questions with the witness so that the witness knows what questions to expect and so the lawyer knows exactly what response the witness will give on examination. The witness at all times must tell the truth, and no lawyer should ever suggest otherwise. But if the lawyer and the witness interpret a question differently, the witness' response may not be what the lawyer expected and could be damaging to your case.

The lawyer also needs to prepare your witnesses for cross-examination by the lawyer for the other side. The lawyer for the other side will be able to ask your witnesses leading questions that suggest their own answers and may even try to trick your witnesses into making a mistake. Your witnesses can not know with certainty what questions the other lawyer will ask them. If your lawyer properly prepares your witnesses for cross-examination, then they should be able to endure the cross-examination with more assurance and self-confidence.

You do not want an overly anxious witness. Unless the witness is a party to the lawsuit, you can assume that the witness does not want to be in your trial. Most witnesses would rather not be missing work and do not like the adversary nature of a trial. They seem to like preparing for the trial, because they are searching for some assurance of what will happen at the trial. Preparing the testimony and the witnesses for trial can be time-consuming. But it is important since it will make the experience of your witnesses less onerous and will make your witnesses more credible in the eyes of the jury.

Documents present different and difficult problems. Your lawyer cannot just waive a document in front of the jury and present it into evidence. Instead, each document must be authenticated. Authentication is the process by which the document is identified in such a way that it is considered reliable information.

Normally, a document is authenticated by the testimony of the person who prepared or signed it. For example, you could identify and authenticate the real estate sales contract or the mortgage that you signed in connection with your real estate case. You could not authenticate a list of events that you prepared for your lawyer several months after the transaction. You may be able to identify it, but you could not convince the court that it would be sufficiently reliable to be presented to the jury.

94

The process of preparing evidence requires that your lawyer be thoroughly familiar with all of the information gathered before this stage and have a complete understanding of how the information will work together at trial.

EVIDENCE MOTIONS

In connection with preparing your evidence, your lawyer needs to review the other party's evidence. As mentioned above, some information never becomes evidence, because it is either unreliable or irrelevant. Sometimes, there are major disagreements over which pieces of information can be presented to the jury. It is the job of your lawyer to prevent unreliable or irrelevant information from being presented to the jury.

If your lawyer believes that the other side will try to present this type of information, he or she should bring a motion to exclude that evidence. These motions are made at or shortly before the start of the trial and are sometimes known as motions in limine. Your lawyer will have to prepare these motions for each type of improper evidence that he believes the other side will try to present. He also

95

will have to be ready to oppose these types of motions that he expects the other side to make. Some courts have a pretrial conference at which these types of motions are considered. Other courts do not have a formal pretrial conference. They will consider these motions at the beginning of the trial usually before the jury is chosen by the attorneys.

Courts are very careful when determining what evidence will be presented to a jury. If your case does not have a jury, the judge will usually be more lenient in allowing improper evidence to be presented. Most judges have the training to recognize improper evidence and will allow it to be presented, since they will attribute the proper amount of weight it deserves in making their decisions.

FOCUSING ARGUMENTS

Your lawyer places the pieces of the puzzle together for the jury so it can see a complete picture, or at least it can see clearly the portion of the picture that you want it to see. By focusing on the arguments that you want to make, your lawyer can, by the use of words, focus the jury's attention on the information that you feel is most important and how that information should be viewed.

Throughout the preparation for trial and the trial itself, your lawyer must keep your position in focus. If you or your lawyer lose this focus, you may end up appearing to be meandering through the lawsuit. It is critical to present your case in an easily understandable and concise way.

THE TRIAL BRIEF

A trial brief is a document that can be presented to the judge at or before the beginning of the trial. The trial brief sets forth the basic issues in the case, each party's positions on the various issues, and the evidence you intend to present to prove your case. Usually, the judge does not require that trial briefs be filed, but lawyers will file them in all but the simplest of cases.

Your lawyer needs to be familiar with the significant issues in the case and understand the positions that all the other parties have taken on the various issues. This may not be difficult if there are few parties and if they are all involved in the same issues. Many cases have numerous defendants, and many of those defendants do not have any interest in all of the issues. In some cases no party, including the plaintiff, is involved in all of the issues in the case.

Your lawyer also needs to be secure in what each of your witnesses will say at trial. If your lawyer tells the judge in the trial brief that he will present certain evidence and then does not, the judge will know that certain facts changed or a claim cannot be supported by appropriate evidence. For that reason, many lawyers describe only the crucial evidence in the trial brief. Deciding what evidence is crucial is not always as simple as it may seem.

Everyone knows that certain information is crucial. For example, in your traffic accident case, the color of the traffic light at the time each car entered the intersection clearly is important. However, information about the time of day, the weather, the road condition or the condition of the cars before the accident may or may not be important. Most lawyers are regularly surprised at what information judges and juries will consider important and this is why some lawyers will present all of their information to the jury. It is not always possible to determine what will become important and change a juror's mind.

The trial brief may also contain legal arguments concerning evidence problems that your lawyer will anticipate when certain evidence is presented at trial. Even if the judge does not decide before trial to exclude certain information, that does not mean that all of that information will be admitted into the case. Depending upon the information that you are trying to present and the way in which it is being presented, the judge may decide not to allow the information into trial.

Finally, your attorney may include legal arguments regarding various points of law involved in the case. Many lawyers will not include the legal arguments, either regarding evidence or other points of law, in their main trial brief. These issues often are included in separate briefs that will deal only with one issue.

THE OPENING STATEMENTS

The opening statement is the method by which your lawyer describes the setting of the dispute, identifies all of the parties and recounts the facts. During the opening statement your lawyer will tell the jury who all the parties are and what information will be presented by each party.

99

This is not the time when your lawyer argues your case. This is the time when your lawyer sets the stage so that the jury can follow the information as it is presented to them.

If your case does not have a jury, the opening statement will be made to the judge. Since the judge has read parts of the pleadings and the trial briefs, the opening statement presented to the judge usually will be shorter than an opening statement presented to a jury. Some lawyers may not present an opening statement to a judge. Sometimes the judge will indicate that opening statements are not necessary. Although you always want to present an opening statement, if the judge indicates that he or she does not want to hear one, prudence may dictate that you not present one.

An opening statement is not just a restatement of the trial brief. Although they cover the same information, the opening statement needs to advise the jury as to the particular facts of the case. A skillfully prepared opening statement will prepare the jury to hear your case. It can paint the various parties as either "good or bad guys." It can engender sympathy or empathy for you or your claims. It tells the jurors what the structure of the puzzle is and how the pieces will be presented as a whole. That way, when the jurors are presented with pieces of the puzzle during the trial they will know where to place them.

There are probably hundreds of books describing different techniques for opening statements. For our purposes, you need to appreciate that, whatever technique your lawyer uses, he or she must analyze the information available, keep his or her focus on what you want to prove, be sensitive to the needs and interests of the jurors and present your case as a story that the jurors can become interested in and care about. This is also the stage at which your lawyer first tries to create a bond between himself or herself, you and the jurors.

CLOSING ARGUMENTS

The closing argument is presented after the jurors have heard all of the evidence. This is the time that your lawyer takes the evidence that has been presented and argues the facts that the jurors have seen and heard and demand that they decide in your favor. This is the time when your lawyer uses all of his or her talents to persuade the judge or the jury that you should win.

Some lawyers prepare their closing arguments early in the case. If your lawyer does this, his or her closing argument will undergo change as new or unexpected information is uncovered. The lawyers who do this argue that the closing argument is the best outline of what they need to prove in the case, so they use it as a guide in preparing their cases for trial.

Whether prepared early or during trial preparation, the closing argument tells the jury not only what you need to prove but also argues that you have proved all of the facts. It also points out the weaknesses and inconsistencies of the other side's case. All significant issues in the case must be covered. In complex cases, the closing argument for each party can take a day or more.

JURY INSTRUCTIONS

Before preparing jury instructions, you and your lawyer must decide if you want a jury. If any party requests a jury and pays the jury fees, and if the case is an appropriate one for a jury, then there will be a jury. Wait a minute. Doesn't the Constitution guarantee you a trial by jury? What kind of case is not appropriate for a jury? After all, juries decide complicated and long cases; what is not appropriate for them to decide?

Remember in Chapter 2 when we discussed the difference between matters of law and matters of equity? Well, juries do not generally decide issues of equity. If you sue somebody for breach of contract and you want to recover damages, your case can be decided by a jury. If you sue that person to stop them from doing some wrongful act (for example, stealing your customers), then your case will be decided by the judge, not by a jury. In those cases in which matters of both equity and law are involved, the jury will decide the matters of law, but only the judge will decide the matters of equity.

Many considerations are involved in the decision of whether to request a jury. Juries are composed of individuals. All of those individuals have their own backgrounds, personalities and prejudices. Most juries consist of twelve people, although some juries are as small as six jurors. Most people are familiar with the requirement in criminal trials that all jurors must agree in order to render a decision. There must be unanimity among the jurors. One juror can, therefore, prevent a verdict. The decision by the jurors is known as the verdict. By the way, the Constitutional right to a trial by jury only applies to criminal trials.

A jury in a civil case does not have to have unanimous agreement of the jurors to render a verdict.

The states vary, but most states require that nine or ten of the jurors agree in order to render a verdict. The decision of whether to request a jury involves an analysis of whether the different backgrounds, personalities and prejudices will be better for you and your case.

If the driver that hit you in your traffic accident case was badly and permanently injured and scarred from the accident, most likely, he or she will want a jury. This is because most people will feel sorry for a badly scarred person. That should not be the basis for their verdict, but it gives the other driver a head start in the case.

In your real estate case, if the person that sold your house to you is a major developer, you may want a jury, because most people prefer the "little guy" over the large corporate "looter." Again, the fact that the seller is rich and powerful should not be the basis for a verdict, but do you really want to throw away that little advantage?

The most significant event in selecting a jury is to remove jurors from the jury panel. You remove a prospective juror from the jury panel by requesting that the judge remove the juror from the panel. You can have the juror removed for cause, or you can exercise what is called a peremptory challenge to the seating of the juror on the panel. To have a prospective juror removed for cause is usually fairly simple, if you have dredged up sufficient information in your questioning of the juror to show some likely prejudice, he or she can be removed for cause.

If a juror happens to be the brother-in-law of one of the parties or the minister of one of the lawyers or has sat on an earlier jury in a trial involving one of the parties, the juror may be removed for cause because there is some likelihood that the juror would allow his decision in the case to be influenced by considerations other than the evidence presented at the trial.

A peremptory challenge is the process of removing a juror from the jury panel without cause. You need not state any reason why you want to remove the juror. Also, you are only allowed a limited number of peremptory challenges. The local court rules will determine how many you may exercise. Often the judge has discretion to decide how many peremptory challenges will be allowed in your case.

Jury trials are a valued tradition, and jury selection is the first time during which you can develop some rapport with the jurors. Through your questions, you can even present to the jurors a flavor for the lawsuit. Through incompetent questioning or intentional abuse of the system, jury selection can take on a greater role in the trial than is necessary. In some cases, the selection of a jury takes longer than the whole rest of the trial.

Some lawyers argue that a trial is won or lost at the time of jury selection. In the overall scheme of events, jury selection is preliminary skirmishing. Very important skirmishing, but a preliminary skirmish nonetheless.

Once a jury is sworn in by the judge, you cannot remove a person from the jury. From then on, only death or illness removes a juror from the panel. Even if there is some juror misconduct during the trial, that juror is not selectively removed. The entire jury panel is excused, and you start again.

All lawyers wonder at some verdicts by juries. Occasionally, juries make decisions which cannot be anticipated by a lawyer. Most of the time, verdicts are well considered by the jurors. Most jurors take their time to consider the information presented at trial. They may not reach the same conclusion that you may reach, but that is one of the risks of taking your case to trial.

Once the decision is made to have a jury, jury instructions must be prepared. These are usually given to the jury by the judge after all of the evidence has been presented. Normally, though, they must be presented to the judge and agreed upon before the trial starts. Jury instructions are the rules of law that apply to your case.

In your traffic accident case, the rules of law relating to the elements of negligence will be presented to the jury. There may be many different statements of the rules relating to negligence. Both sides will prepare proposed jury instructions regarding the different elements of negligence. If the proposed jury instructions prepared by each side differ, the judge will decide which one to use after hearing argument from each side.

In your traffic accident case, there is an issue of whether the other driver could have avoided the accident even though you turned in front of her. The jury instructions prepared by your lawyer will have the rules of law relating to comparative fault or contributory negligence, depending on which of those theories is recognized in your state.

Either at a pretrial conference or at the beginning of trial before the jury is selected, the judge will review all of the jury instructions that have been proposed by the lawyers. After listening to any argument that the lawyers make regarding the various proposed instructions, the judge will decide which rules of law will be read to the jury.

The preparation of jury instructions is very important, because the judge will use those instructions to tell the jurors what the law is so they can apply the law to the facts. The jury's job is to decide what facts are supported by the evidence. As long as there are some facts presented at the trial to support the verdict, jurors are given wide discretion to decide what set of facts to believe in a trial. Among the facts that they believe, they can also decide how important those facts are and how much weight to attribute to them. Jurors, however, do not decide what the law is and what laws should be applied to the case.

The judge is the only one who makes all the legal rulings in your case. The lawyers may propose rulings, but it is the judge's duty to make the rulings. Therefore, the judge will tell the jury what the law is as it applies to the facts that the jury chooses to believe in your case.

Some states have published standard jury instructions. Obviously, this makes your lawyer's job easier. Published jury instructions will not apply to unusual rules of law. So your lawyer will still have to perform substantial research on some of the proposed instructions. Although courts have a preference for using standard jury instructions, when they are available, your lawyer should not be afraid to propose a nonstandard instruction, if there has been a recent change or if a different rule would be more applicable to the facts of your particular case.

SETTLEMENT POSSIBILITIES

It is a fact that almost all cases settle without proceeding to trial. It also is a fact that most of those cases that settle do so within the last few days or weeks before trial, sometimes on the day of the trial itself.

From a client's perspective, you may not want your lawyer to fully prepare the case any earlier than is absolutely necessary, because you are sure the case will not proceed to trial. From a lawyer's perspective, it may be necessary to fully prepare your case before the last minute since most lawyers are very busy and tend to jump from crisis to crisis.

Interestingly enough, though, the better prepared you and your lawyer are, the better the chances of settlement. Knowing that some lawyers are procrastinators, your lawyer may be able to dazzle the opposing lawyer at a settlement conference with the amount of information that you have lined up on your side and with the completeness of the research that your lawyer has done for the settlement conference. Such a display may encourage the other lawyer to begin work on his or her case; it may also discourage him or her. If you or your lawyer become discouraged with your case, you need to settle it.

Many courts will help you try to settle your case. During the time for trial preparation, the court may schedule a mandatory settlement conference. All lawyers and clients must attend. If it is conducted by an experienced settlement judge, everyone will be harangued and everyone's case belittled. If the judge makes the parties see the weaknesses of their own cases, then the parties are more likely to settle.

Remember, settlements occur when the parties perceive that the cost to settle the case is less than the cost to continue the case. The cost to continue the case includes the possibility of an adverse judgment. The hardest case to settle is the one where one of the parties does not believe that he or she has anything to lose.

There may be any number of reasons that so many settlements occur on the day the trial is scheduled to start. Some parties get "cold feet"; they either do not want to

110

testify in court or they are afraid of the outcome. Some lawyers, once they have fully prepared the case for trial, may realize they cannot win the case.

The courts that have mandatory settlement conferences do not conduct them for the altruistic purpose of bringing people together and healing broken relationships (except maybe in matters involving marriages and children). The judges know that every case that settles will open up a courtroom for a few hours or a few days. Courtrooms in some places are at a premium. So these courts conduct settlement conferences, in part, as a matter of self-preservation. Whether courts conduct settlement conferences for altruistic or economic reasons, the net effect is the same; you are pressured to settle your case.

Whether or not your court system has mandatory settlement conferences, during trial preparation, you and your lawyer need to continue to evaluate the possibilities of settling your case. If you do not initiate settlement discussions, you must be prepared to respond to settlement requests. This is the most likely time during your case that you will have serious settlement requests.

111

CHAPTER 8

THE TRIAL

Now it is time for. . . **The Trial**. After some injury or damage has occurred, after the results of your investigation and legal research have been amassed, after pleadings have been filed, after discovery has been completed, after all the pretrial motions have been presented and argued, after all settlement negotiations have been exhausted, and after all of the trial preparation has been completed, then, and only then, is it time for The Trial. The trial is your day in court.

You have now arrived at Western civilization's substitute for the duel. You have waited several months, in some places several years, to go to trial. You are pumped up emotionally as a result of the combination of adrenaline pumping through your system and of your fear of the unfamiliar. You have summoned all of your faculties to

113

concentrate on this one battle, because you know that you must out-think and out-maneuver your opponent. You must carry out your tactics with the skill of a seasoned battlefield commander or a championship chess player. And what will you do for most of the day? Sit and wait.

COURT CONGESTION

A trial in an American court is a highly-focused, highly-structured battle. With a single exception (that you are unlikely to be personally injured by the other party), a trial has all of the attributes of a well-planned encounter on the field of battle. It carries with it all of the danger and excitement of risking total failure in order to attempt total victory. Sometimes the stakes are not high, but sometimes they involve a party's livelihood, his ability to feed his family or pay for needed and long-term medical treatment. Sometimes at stake is a party's personal honor and integrity.

With all of this intensity growing within you as you approach the trial, you have to deal with one of the realities of modern life: court congestion. In all metropolitan areas,

114

and in many other parts of the country, courts are crowded. There are more people waiting to go to trial than there are courtrooms available to handle those trials.

Whatever its causes, court congestion affects you when you go to trial, because you may spend several hours or several days waiting for your trial to start. A short mention should be made of the two main methods for handling cases. In one system, one judge handles the entire lawsuit from beginning to end. That judge sets up the trial date presumably with some notion of whether he or she will be available on that date. This is the system used by the federal courts. Of course, if a trial handled by the judge is longer than anticipated (which is not an unusual circumstance), then the next trial, or the next several trials, may be delayed.

The other method for handling cases is known as the master calendar method. All of the cases scheduled to start their trials are assigned to a presiding judge. Many times, the presiding judge is more an administrator than a judge. The presiding judge assigns trials to all other courtrooms in the courthouse. When a courtroom becomes available for a civil trial, the presiding judge assigns the next case to that courtroom.

Typically, more cases are scheduled for trial on a given day than the number of trials that can start right away. You may wait around for several hours or days before your case is either assigned to a courtroom or continued to some new trial date in the future. The presiding judge will not allow you to leave, since he or she needs you in court and ready to proceed as soon as a courtroom becomes available.

Each of these methods has its benefits, but neither is without its flaws. You will find many variations within each method. And a number of states are experimenting with various methods in an effort to accelerate the entire litigation process, including proceeding to trial. The issues of economy and efficiency of courts are a growing concern to the legislatures, the courts themselves and to the public. Because of that, you will probably encounter increasing efforts to resolve your case, in some manner, without going to trial.

MOTIONS IN LIMINE

Often the first event in a trial, especially if it is scheduled for more than one day, is for the lawyers and the judge to meet face to face. This may happen in the courtroom, but it often happens in the judge's chambers. Most of the time, the parties to the lawsuit are not directly involved in this meeting, unless they are representing themselves. The reason for the meeting is to set forth the ground rules for the trial. The basic format of all trials is the same, but each judge has his or her own individual way of handling matters.

At this meeting, the judge will hear motions in limine. This phrase simply means motions made at the beginning, or on the threshold, of the trial. These motions usually have to do with expected evidence problems. A judge can decide at this time whether certain types of evidence will be allowed, so you can proceed through the trial with the confidence of knowing what type of evidence you can present and what type of evidence the other side will not be able to present to the court.

Even though evidence comes in little discreet pieces of information, these pieces do not exist in isolation. Often you will ask several questions of a witness for the sole purpose of setting up the presentation of a critical piece of information. If you do not find out until you ask the critical question that the judge will not allow that information to be presented as evidence, you will be frustrated, and the jury may be distracted. A motion in limine can avoid that problem.

A judge will make several rulings on evidence questions throughout the trial. When an objection is made to evidence that one party is trying to present in the trial, the judge will rule on it either immediately or following a brief argument. If you have a particularly difficult evidence problem, you may want to address it at the beginning of the trial. You will have the judge's complete attention on this issue at that time. Later, a judge may not be able to give your evidence question as much time and effort as you would like under the circumstances.

Arguments over evidence questions never take place in front of the jury. If the judge wants to entertain argument on an evidence question during the trial, one of two things will happen. Occasionally, if an evidence question is a major issue that will take significant argument, the jury will be taken from the courtroom while the parties argue over the objection to the evidence. Most often, arguments over evidence last only a few moments and take place at what is called a side bar conference.

A side bar conference includes all parties to the lawsuit or their lawyers, the judge and the court reporter. It takes place to the side of the bench where the judge sits farthest from the jury. These conferences are conducted in whispers, so the jury should not hear what is said. The court reporter, however, takes down everything that is said.

118

Once the judge makes his or her decision, all the parties, the judge and the court reporter resume their places in the courtroom, and the judge announces what the decision is regarding the objection that was made to the evidence.

JURY SELECTION

After the pretrial administrative matters and the motions in limine are completed, the trial begins. The first event is the selection of a jury. Not all civil cases have juries. The Constitutional right to trial by jury only applies to criminal cases. Long before you proceed to trial, you have to request a jury and post jury fees, if you want a jury. The selection of juries was discussed in Chapter 7.

OPENING STATEMENTS

The opening statement is the second of only three times that the lawyers speak directly to the jury: jury selection, opening statement and closing argument. The nature of an opening statement was described in Chapter

119

7. All opening statements are given by the parties only if they are representing themselves. Otherwise, they are given by the lawyers.

The plaintiff gives his opening statement first, then each defendant, in turn, gives his opening statement. An opening statement can be as short as a few minutes or as long as the judge will allow. You will not argue your case in your opening statement, but you want to make sure that you give the jury an idea as to what to expect from the presentation of your case.

PLAINTIFF'S CASE

Following the opening statements, the plaintiff presents his case to the judge or the jury. Finally, the plaintiff begins to place the puzzle pieces -- those pieces of information known as evidence -- before the trier of fact. Remember, the judge will decide what facts to believe if there is no jury. Otherwise, the jury will make those decisions. We will assume that a jury is hearing your case.

How is evidence presented to the jury? There are two primary types of evidence: oral testimony and documentary evidence. Occasionally, a jury will view a videotape or listen to an audiotape or visit the scene of a crime or an accident, but most evidence consists of either the words of a live witness or the review of a document.

Oral Testimony

Oral testimony is presented to the jury through the use of probing questions. The questions themselves are critically important, but they are not evidence. Only the answers of the witness are evidence. Before a witness testifies, he or she is sworn in. From that point on, the witness is obligated to tell the truth at all times during the trial.

If a witness does not tell the truth, he or she may be guilty of the crime of perjury. Perjury, however, is a difficult crime to prove and is not often pursued. So, then, how do you know if the witness is telling the truth? You do not. There are two main controls that govern the truthfulness of witnesses. The first is the tradition in this country of respect for the rule of law and the courts. The entire system of jurisprudence, as practiced in the United States, depends upon the truthfulness of people.

121

The second control is the structure of the trial itself. Both sides in each trial have the opportunity to fully present their cases. Each side can call its own party as a witness, any independent witnesses that it wants and even the adverse party. Sometimes, the testimony of a witness is directly contradicted by one or more other witnesses. The more witnesses you have on your side (assuming that your witnesses are believable), the more weight the jury will give to their stories.

Even more important than directly contradictory evidence is the flavor, or the feel for the events, that the jury has through the testimony of the witnesses. As a number of witnesses testify, the jury starts to have a feel for how events occurred and for how the parties acted. If the jury then hears some testimony that does not fit into that pattern, a conflict is created, and the jurors must resolve that conflict. Most often, human nature will resolve that conflict by discarding the conflicting testimony in favor of the general flow of events. Remember, it is the jury's job to decide who is telling the truth.

If neither of these controls sounds particularly compelling to you, you must keep in mind that this is the nature of the trial. The result is not based on truth and

justice. The result is justice based on the evidence
presented at the trial. This may be the best reason always
to keep settlement options open.

When the plaintiff starts calling witnesses, it is called
direct examination.   The plaintiff cannot ask leading
questions of his witnesses during direct examination. "What
color was the light when you entered the intersection?" and
"Was the light red when you entered the intersection?" are
both legitimate questions. But, "The light was red when
you entered the intersection, wasn't it?" is not a legitimate
question on direct examination. It is a leading question. It
suggests its own answer.

Subject to any objections that the other side might
make to any of the evidence, the plaintiff has complete
control over his or her direct examination. Presumably, he
or she knows what each of his or her witnesses will say.
Most witnesses called during plaintiff's direct examination
will be friendly to the plaintiff's case or else the plaintiff
would not call them as witnesses. In some circumstances,
a plaintiff may want to call the defendant during the
plaintiff's case. This is usually done for tactical reasons,
and the rules of cross-examination apply.

After the plaintiff finishes his or her direct
examination of a witness, each defendant has an
opportunity to cross-examine that witness. The limitations

of direct examination do not apply to cross-examination. The defendant may ask leading questions. In fact, the defendant may ask nearly any type of question that he or she wants so long as it is relevant to the case and it does not harass or badger the witness.

The purpose of direct examination is for the plaintiff to tell his or her story in his or her own manner. The purpose of cross-examination is to punch holes in that story. Through cross-examination, the defendant can expose inconsistencies in the witness' testimony and can cause the witness to disclose evidence damaging to the plaintiff's case. The witness only responds to questions, so the defendant on cross-examination must ask the questions that the plaintiff on direct examination did not ask the witnesses.

A defendant should be able to anticipate the witness' answers on cross-examination. If you ask open-ended questions without anticipating the answers, you may have testimony which is damaging to your own case. There is no dishonor in not conducting cross-examination. If you do not believe you can score some points, or at least clarify a few points, you should not cross-examine a witness.

Cross-examination is critically important. It is also very difficult to do correctly and very dangerous if done incorrectly. Do not expect your cross-examination to produce surprise confessions of guilt. Most cross-examination should produce additional pieces of information for the jury to hear that the plaintiff did not produce. Cross-examination is a powerful tool because of the harm that it can render to a witness' testimony.

Effective cross-examination can lead a witness into a corner where he or she has no alternative to contradicting (or appearing to contradict) earlier testimony. Also, the witnesses' credibility can be attacked.

Following cross-examination, the plaintiff may ask additional questions of the witness in re-direct examination. The purpose of re-direct examination is to clarify issues that have been raised by the cross-examination and to conduct damage control. If the cross-examination has been damaging to the plaintiff's case, the plaintiff can try to rehabilitate the witness in the eyes of the jury.

This process of direct examination followed by cross-examination followed by re-direct examination is followed for each witness. When the plaintiff has called all of his witnesses, the plaintiff will rest his or her case. Following the plaintiff's case, there may be some motions by the defendants claiming that the plaintiff did not prove his or her case and that the plaintiff's case should be dismissed without the need for any witnesses for the defense.

Documentary Evidence

In some cases, documents play an important role. Some lawsuits are decided by the contents of a single document. Still other lawsuits may have hundreds of documents that become part of the jury's consideration. On rare occasions, an entire lawsuit can be decided by documents alone. But documents are not easy to introduce into evidence.

You cannot simply hold up a document in front of the jury and tell the jurors to consider it in their decision. Any document introduced as evidence in a trial must be authenticated. Most documents are authenticated by oral testimony. Some witness must testify that this is the document that he or she signed, prepared, sent or received.

Given the time it takes to go to trial, some witnesses will not recognize a particular document. If there is only one witness who can authenticate a document, you could be in trouble. This is one argument for substantial preliminary investigation at the time that a lawsuit is filed. If you develop your whole case based on a document only to discover at trial that no one can properly authenticate that document, you may have wasted substantial time and money.

126

As an example, let us examine the real estate case. When you first notice damage to your new house shortly after you move in, you review your papers relating to the transaction. Among those papers you find some type of disclosure document apparently from the sellers telling you there are no physical problems with the house. You do not remember where you obtained that document, but there it is. If you cannot identify when and from whom you received that document, then you must rely on the other side to identify this document for you.

If the sellers deny seeing or signing that document, and if the sellers and real estate people deny giving that document to you, you may not be able to have that document introduced into evidence. Unless you have some witness who can identify the signatures or otherwise identify the document, you might as well not have it.

Some documents are presumed to be reliable. For example, if you have a certified copy of a public record, like a birth certificate or a recorded deed to property, then that document can be used as evidence without any oral testimony to authenticate it. Of course, you may need oral testimony to show how a certified document was used, but you do not need that testimony to use the document as evidence.

127

Unless all the parties agree that copies of documents may be used, or unless the original document simply is no longer available, the original document must be used. The original document is the actual document that was prepared. The actual hand written or typed note. The one with the actual signature on it. In most cases, the lawyers are sufficiently familiar with the documents that are likely to be used at trial that they will agree to use copies. If they do not, it could create some problems. The jury is entitled to see the best evidence available, and documentary evidence often stays in a court file for years after a trial is completed.

DEFENDANTS' CASE

Following the end of the plaintiff's case, each defendant, in turn, will present his or her own side of the case. The format for the presentation of evidence is the same for the defendants as it was for the plaintiff. First, a defendant conducts direct examination of a witness. Then the plaintiff and each other defendant can cross-examine the witness. If the defendant feels that it is necessary or desirable, he or she may then conduct re-direct examination in order to clarify the evidence or to try to rehabilitate the witness.

There is one limitation on cross-examination that was not mentioned above. On direct examination, any questions relevant to the issues in the lawsuit may be asked. It is not unusual for the person conducting direct examination to ask questions of a witness dealing with only one subject or just a few subjects. Many witnesses, after all, do not know everything about the case. They are there only to fill in certain parts of the puzzle, not to describe the entire puzzle.

On cross-examination, the witness can only be asked questions that are within the scope of the direct examination. As an example, if a witness is asked on direct examination only if he saw the plaintiff sign a particular document, then he can only be asked on cross-examination about the signing of the document (and, possibly, the circumstances surrounding the actual signing of the document). He cannot be asked on cross-examination about any other aspects of the transaction.

REBUTTAL

After each defendant has presented his case, he rests. After all of the defendants have rested, then the plaintiff has one more chance. If the plaintiff feels that it is necessary, he or she may call more witnesses in an effort to rebut the evidence presented by the defendants. Documents and oral testimony are presented in the same way as before. Since the purpose of this part of the case is to rebut the defendants' evidence, it can only address issues addressed by the defendants. It cannot raise new issues.

Often there is no rebuttal at all in a case. Even if there is rebuttal, it often consists of a handful of questions. Seldom does rebuttal take a significant amount of trial time.

CLOSING ARGUMENTS

After everyone has finished presenting their evidence, each party addresses the jury for the last time. The closing arguments are just that: argument. By

130

presenting evidence, you have already placed all these individual puzzle pieces in front of the jury. This is the time when you make sure that the jurors see the picture that you want them to see.

This is the time when you argue the purity of your motives. This is the time when you argue that the other side is telling a story that should not be believed. This is the time when you argue that the other side's evidence does not mean anything but that your evidence means everything. Whatever point you feel needs to be made should be made clearly during closing arguments.

This is another time when lawyers will act differently depending on whether there is a jury. In front of a jury, a lawyer may tend to be more dramatic and seek sympathy for his or her client. If there is no jury, all lawyers will still make a closing argument to the judge, but he or she will spend more time in the legal issues than on the emotional ones. Any judge who has been on the bench for a few years has heard all of the emotional appeals too many times.

The plaintiff presents the first closing argument. He or she is followed, in turn, by each defendant. After each defendant has completed his or her closing argument, the plaintiff, again, has the final word. This last opportunity for the plaintiff is for the purpose of rebutting some of the

131

argument of the defendants. As with the presentation of testimony, the plaintiff cannot, at this last appeal to the jury, present new arguments or information except in response to something said by the defendants in their closing arguments.

If you have raised the jury's interest in your case in your opening statement, and if you have clearly presented all of your evidence to the jury, you still must present a clear, concise and strong closing argument. Have you ever read a book that held your interest but fell flat in the last two pages? Most likely, you were disappointed. Well, your closing argument is similar to those last two pages. Even if the jurors are on your side, if you do not tell them, clearly and forcefully, why they need too decide for you, they will feel disappointed and unfulfilled.

Do not leave your jurors unfulfilled. A carefully crafted argument can leave the jurors with the impression that they have no alternative but to decide in your favor. It is best to have the jurors start their deliberations with a positive impression about your case.

INSTRUCTIONS TO JURY

Remember during trial preparation one of the items you prepared were proposed jury instructions? And remember that during the conference with the judge at the beginning of the trial, you argued over which instructions would be presented to the jury? Well, now those instructions will be presented to the jury. In some courts, these instructions are given before the closing arguments. The judge always gives these instructions.

The jury acts as a fact finder in a trial. The jurors must determine which facts to believe. The judge tells the jury what law is to be used in analyzing the facts. When a jury deliberates, it decides what the true facts are and then applies the law (as told to them by the judge) to those facts. The jury is free to disbelieve any evidence presented at trial; it is not free to disbelieve the law as presented by the judge. Even if a juror is sure that the law is different from what the judge presents, that juror must still render a decision based on the instructions from the judge.

A judge can include at this time certain findings of fact. Even though the jury is the fact finder, the judge can direct the jurors to make certain findings. This is not often done. It occurs when the judge (who has also listened to all the evidence) determines that no evidence was presented to support or challenge a particular fact. Then, and only then, does the judge instruct the jurors to make particular findings of fact. All other instructions to the jurors consist of the rules of law to be used in deciding this case. Most often, the instructions to the jury are the last item provided to the jurors before they begin their deliberations.

CHAPTER 9

THE DECISION

A trial is a dynamic process that pulls you one way for a while and then pushes you in the other direction. There are times when you will wonder how you ever thought you could win this lawsuit. Then there are other times when you cannot conceive how you could lose. After all the evidence is presented, after the closing arguments and instructions to the jury, the most dynamic part of the trial takes place, but you will not see any of it.

Jurors all approach their task differently. Some jurors take copious notes and organize their thoughts meticulously. Others seem to be ruled by the general feel that they have for the parties to the lawsuit. However they approach their decision, the deliberations are a study in group psychology. You have twelve people who, before this

135

trial, may never have met each other. They spend a few hours, days or weeks listening to you and your opponent fight in court during which time they are not supposed to discuss the case even among themselves. Then they are told what rules of law to apply and to decide who wins.

They meet together, in private, and discuss the various aspects of the case. They try to reach a consensus regarding each issue and try to reach a final decision. The foreperson of the jury will be asked in open court what the decision of the jury is, but each juror may well be asked if he or she agrees with that verdict, so the jurors cannot hide behind the anonymity of the group.

Generally, a verdict will state who wins and how much that party should receive in damages. Sometimes, a jury will be asked to make special verdicts -- a verdict by which the jury discloses whether it found certain facts to be true. As an example, a jury in your traffic accident case could be asked to make a special verdict on whether the light was red when you entered the intersection. That issue, by itself, may not decide your case, but unless you request this special verdict, you will not know what finding the jury made on that issue. Special verdicts are usually reserved for issues of critical importance to the outcome or to issues that may become the basis for an appeal.

Not only do you not observe this exercise in group decision-making, you have no control over what happens in the deliberations. You also have no idea as to what the jurors thought was important. The jurors may spend hours arguing over some point that nobody else thought was important. But to those twelve jurors, or at least to some of them, it is very important.

Depending on the nature of the lawsuit, how long the trial was and the motivation of the jurors, a decision could be reached in a few minutes or not for several days or weeks. Once the jury has reached a decision, the foreperson tells the court bailiff who then tells the judge. The court clerk then calls all parties and their lawyers into court. Only then will the jury come back into the jury box and announce its decision. Usually the decision is written on a verdict form and given to the court clerk who then reads the verdict.

If the jury decides in your favor, you may think you have just experienced the ultimate vindication, but restrain your celebration. What you need is the ruling of the court, not the verdict of the jury. The judge has the authority to adopt the verdict and issue a judgment in the case based on the verdict. However, the judge also has the authority to overturn the verdict and issue a judgment in the case that is contrary to the findings of the jury. This is called a judgment notwithstanding the verdict.

137

Most judges have great respect for the jury system, so they do not overturn verdicts very often. A judge only overturns a verdict if there was insufficient evidence to support the verdict. The judge cannot substitute his or her own belief of what evidence is true for that of the jurors. He or she can, however, decide that there simply was not enough evidence presented at the trial to sustain the verdict (or a particular finding by the jury).

The judgment usually will be issued immediately after the jury has declared its verdict. Sometimes, especially in complex cases or in cases where the verdict is not what the judge expected to hear, the judge may wait a few days before entering a judgment in the case. This extra few days gives the judge an opportunity to review and understand the verdict and to determine if it should be overturned. A jury verdict will be overturned by the judge only when it is very clear to the judge that the verdict needs to be overturned.

Everyone goes into court expecting that he or she will win and the other side will lose. Most often that is the case. Most lawsuits result in one winner and one loser. A jury must make its findings based on the evidence presented at trial, but that evidence is filtered through the life experiences of each of the jurors. In a case in which there is clearly no evil person, it is human nature to want to see both people win. We sometimes receive what seem to be compromise decisions.

It is improper for jurors to intentionally work out a compromise decision, but it is not too difficult in some cases to find that neither side wins on all issues. In those cases, juries will sometimes decide in favor of one party but for much less than that party was seeking in damages. In one major products liability case a few years ago, a jury ruled in favor of the plaintiff but awarded her no damages whatsoever. So, the uncertainties of trial continue into the verdict and judgment stages of the trial.

A word should be mentioned about the judgment if the trial is conducted with no jury. Most trials are fairly short, and many judges take many notes during trial. Many of those judges will issue their judgments right after the end of closing arguments. If a judge does this, he or she often will make specific findings of fact, so the basis for the judgment is clear. If the judge, sitting without a jury, does not rule right away, he or she will take the case under submission.

When a judge takes a case under submission, he or she will study his or her notes and prepare a judgment when he or she is ready to rule. Occasionally, you may have to wait a long time before the judge issues the

139

judgment, and it is possible that the judgment, when issued, will have no findings or explanation. If the judge makes no written findings, it may be more difficult to understand how the judgment was reached. It also may be somewhat more difficult to appeal the judgment, if you feel that is necessary.

Findings are always desirable but not always necessary. Unless the local court rules require that findings be made, the judge may have no obligation to make them. In some courts, you may have to specifically request, before the trial, that findings be made.

During a lawsuit, you should not speak with the judge or the jurors about the lawsuit without the other parties or their lawyers present. After the trial, however, there is no reason why you cannot speak either with the judge or the jurors. Although not common, it is not unheard of for a lawyer to approach the judge after the trial is over for a critique of how the lawyer fared in the trial. It is very common for lawyers to approach jurors after a trial to discuss the case.

Lawyers want to know what was important to the jurors. This is the only time that the lawyers can find out this information. Jurors certainly are not obligated to talk to the lawyers or any parties to the lawsuit, but many of them seem happy to do so. Often, they have their own questions that they want answered. Jurors are usually aware that some information was not presented to them for some reason. They just seem to know that they have not seen the entire puzzle, so they often ask questions after the trial to fill in the missing pieces.

By talking to the jurors after the trial, lawyers can find out what type of witnesses were effective and what tactics or techniques worked. If you approach jurors openly they will tell you what they liked or did not like about your case and, even, what they liked or did not like about you. These conversations with the judge or jury after trial are not an official part of the legal proceedings, but they can be quite educational. They can be the only opportunity to find out how the decision-makers are affected by the proceedings in a trial.

CHAPTER 10

FOLLOWING TRIAL

Congratulations! You have survived the long and sometimes gruelling task of proceeding with a lawsuit. And you have won. The jury issued its verdict in your favor. The judge entered the judgment in your favor. You have been vindicated. The court said that you were right. Even better, if the court awarded you damages, you can now start to collect them from the other side. Well...maybe.

Believe it or not, this lawsuit still may not finished. The losing party may bring a motion for reconsideration or for a new trial. Or, just when you thought that you were done with this lawsuit, the losing party could file an appeal.

MOTION FOR RECONSIDERATION

A motion for reconsideration is made to the trial court and is heard by the same judge who presided over the case. A motion for reconsideration basically argues that the judgment of the court was somehow against the rule of law or not supported by the law. If this motion is made, you must respond to it, in writing, setting forth why you think the judgment that was entered is supported by the law.

Since this motion is being heard by the same judge who entered the judgment, and since the moving party is asking that judge to rule that the judgment was in error, these motions are not often granted. Still, you have to deal with these motions. It takes time and effort to make or oppose a motion for reconsideration. The time, effort and expense you spend in opposing this motion is not generally recoverable as part of your judgment, but you must oppose this motion. If you do not, you could find your hard-earned judgment will disappear.

MOTION FOR A NEW TRIAL

A motion for a new trial is also made to the trial court. However, the basis for this motion is quite different from the basis for a motion for reconsideration. A motion for new trial can be granted if the moving party has new evidence that was not presented at the trial. The new evidence has to be newly-discovered evidence that could not reasonably have been known to the moving party at the time of trial.

If the evidence was available to the moving party at the trial, then it cannot be the basis for a motion for a new trial. The most blatant example of new evidence that would support this motion is a surprise witness who surfaces only after the trial. The moving party is not asking the judge to overturn his or her own earlier judgment, as in the motion for reconsideration, but because the evidence to support this motion cannot have been available to the moving party at the trial, this motion, also, is seldom granted.

Motions for reconsideration and motions for a new trial are often made as a procedural matter on technical grounds. When these motions are denied, they then can become another basis for an appeal.

APPEAL

If the losing party feels that the judgment is not supported by the evidence or that some error was made in the trial itself, then he or she may appeal to a higher court. Usually the errors that parties complain of are rulings by the judge on some question of evidence. The appellant (the party filing the appeal) claims that the judge either allowed in evidence that should not have been presented or prevented some evidence that should have been presented. Whatever the basis for the appeal, the appellant must show that he or she was denied a fair trial or his or her position in the lawsuit was somehow prejudiced by the error.

An appeal can be a time-consuming and costly affair. I have seen cases settle after judgment in order to keep an appeal from being filed. The appeal process is ridiculously easy to start, but the first step is the last easy part of an appeal. After a notice of appeal is filed with the trial court, all sorts of time limits start. Each party must designate which pleadings from the lawsuit file and which part of the evidence presented at trial he or she wants designated in the appeal court file. Designating the file can be an exhausting task in a complex case. It also costs money for the clerk and the court reporter to reproduce the documents and the testimony.

After the various parts of the file are designated, the appellant has a certain amount of time within which to file the appellant's brief. Making reference to the evidence presented at trial, the appellant's brief contains all the legal arguments why something that occurred at the trial was in error and how it prejudiced the case. After the appellant's brief is filed, the respondent (the party against whom the appeal is filed) has a certain amount of time within which to file a respondent's brief containing all the legal arguments why no error was made or, if one was made, why no prejudice occurred.

The appellant has one more opportunity to file a reply brief responding to any issues raised in the respondent's brief. After all the briefs have been filed, the court of appeal will review everything that has been filed with it. The court of appeal may order oral arguments. Ultimately, the court of appeal can decide whether the judgment can remain as entered by the trial judge, whether the judgment must be overturned or whether the whole

147

case should have a new trial. A new trial could be ordered on all issues or on only one issue.

There are many specific and technical requirements for appeals that are beyond the scope of this book. The point is that your lawsuit can reach far beyond the end of the trial before it is concluded.

CONCLUSION

If you have read through this whole book, you may be wondering why anyone resorts to litigation to resolve disputes. Certainly not all lawsuits carry with them all of the problem areas mentioned in this book. But you never have complete control over what problem areas may arise in a given case.

As mentioned in the Introduction, this is not a book intended to guide you through your own lawsuit. It is intended to familiarize you with the system. If you find yourself unwillingly involved in a lawsuit, or if you are contemplating starting a lawsuit, you should know as much as you can about the process you are entering. The less surprised you are at the various twists and turns a lawsuit can take, the more effectively you will be able to concentrate on the substantive issues involved in your case. Remember, all of the procedures that seem so foreign to you are designed to produce the truth on the substantive issues.

This book is not for lawyers. I imagine most lawyers will find it simplistic. This book is for you, the party, the participant, the plaintiff or defendant. I have tried to make the process of proceeding through a lawsuit a little less fearsome. I trust that, after reading this book, you will find it so.

GLOSSARY
(Nonlegal Definitions Of Legal Terms)

ACTUAL DAMAGES. Damages that are awarded to a plaintiff to compensate him for his actual and real loss or injury. These damages are the same as general damages.

ADMINISTRATOR. A man appointed by the court to handle the affairs of another person or company. An administrator collects assets, pays debts and distributes what is left over as ordered by the court.

ADMINISTRATRIX. A woman administrator.

APPEAL. The review by an appellate court of the final ruling made by a lower court in which the appellate court is asked to correct some error or reverse the judgment of the lower court. The lower court must have made a final judgment in the case, and there must be an appellate court.

APPELLATE COURTS. A court that has the authority to review the decisions of other courts. Not a trial court or a court that has original jurisdiction (except under special circumstances).

AUTHENTICATION. The method by which a written document is shown to be authentic, so it can be admitted as evidence.

BENCH. The seat in court occupied by the judge. Also refers to the judges of a court as distinguished from the lawyers who are called the bar.

BENEFICIARY. A person for whose benefit a trust is created. A person who enjoys the benefits of some property that is under the legal control of another person (such as a trustee, executor, etc.).

BREACH OF WARRANTY. A warranty is an affirmative promise in a contract, so a breach of warranty is the failure or falsehood of that promise. Breach of warranty is not the same as fraud and does not require that the party breaking the promise has some guilty knowledge that the promise is false.

CHAMBERS. A judge's office.

CIRCUIT COURT OF APPEAL. The federal court system is divided into eleven judicial circuits. The circuit courts of appeal are the appellate courts in each circuit.

CIVIL MATTER. A matter in which somebody seeks to recover some civil right or to obtain recovery for some wrong that is not a crime. Civil matters relate to and affect only individual rights; criminal matters involve wrongs against the public.

COMPLAINT. The first pleading filed by a plaintiff in a civil matter. It is intended to give the defendant information of the material facts upon which the plaintiff bases his demand.

CONSEQUENTIAL DAMAGES. Damages that do not flow directly and immediately from a wrongful act, but flow only from some of the consequences or results of a wrongful act. If somebody wrongfully wrecks your car that you use in business, the repair of your car flows directly and immediately from the wrongful act. Your loss of income while your car is being repaired is the result of a consequence of the wrongful act.

153

CONSERVATOR. A person who protects and preserves the estate of another. If somebody is found by a court to be incapable of handling his own affairs, the court shall appoint a conservator to manage the affairs of the incapable person.

CRIMINAL MATTER. An action brought by the state against a person charged with a public offense for the purpose of punishing that person.

DEFENDANT. The person against whom a lawsuit is brought.

DEMURRER. A claim by a defendant that she should not be required to answer the complaint. The defendant claims that, even if all of the allegations in the complaint are true, they are not adequate to require the defendant to have to answer them.

DEPOSITION. As used in this book, oral testimony by a person under oath before a court reporter (but not in court) and taken down in writing by the court reporter.

DIRECT DAMAGES. This is not really a legal term. It is used in this book to mean the same thing as special damages.

154

DISAGREEMENT. Some difference of opinion. Some lack of uniformity or concurrence in the way different people view something.

DISCOVERY. The process, enforceable by the court, to secure evidence that is in the other party's possession.

DIVERSITY JURISDICTION. A phrase used to describe the jurisdiction that federal courts have to hear a case when all of the persons on one side of a lawsuit must be citizens of different states from all the persons on the other side of the lawsuit.

ENVIRONMENTAL IMPACT REPORT. A report showing the effects on the environment of a particular project and addressing various methods of mitigating those effects. Most government agencies are required to review and approve an environmental impact report before a project can be approved.

EQUITABLE REMEDIES. Remedies that do not seek the recovery of damages, but rather the enforcement of some other right. In old English law and in a few states, these remedies are enforceable only in special courts of equity.

155

EQUITY MATTERS. Matters that involve the resolution of some right other than the recovery of damages. If you sue on a promissory note, you seek damages; but if you sue to foreclose on the property used as security for the promissory note, you seek equity.

ESCROW. The process by which a document is given to a third person to hold until certain conditions are met. When those conditions are met, the escrow holder is obligated to transfer the document to somebody else. An escrow is often used in real estate transactions.

EVIDENCE. Any bits of information presented legally at trial through witnesses, records, documents, objects, etc. Evidence is presented by a party to a lawsuit for the purpose of inducing the judge or jury to believe the story presented by that party.

EXECUTOR. A person appointed by somebody in that person's will to dispose of that person's property according to the terms of the will, after that person dies.

EXECUTRIX. A female executor.

FEDERAL JUDGES. An officer nominated by the President and approved by the Senate who presides over a court in the federal court system. A federal judge's appointment cannot be terminated except by death, voluntary retirement or by impeachment.

FELONY. Generally, a felony is a crime that is punishable by death or by imprisonment in a penitentiary for more than one year. Felonies are more serious than misdemeanors.

FIDUCIARY. A person having a duty to act primarily for the benefit of another in relation to a particular matter. The fiduciary acts as a trustee and owes the beneficiary of that relationship scrupulous good faith and candor.

FORFEITURE. The loss of some right or property as a punishment for a crime or delinquency. In this sense, forfeiture is frequently associated with the word "penalty".

FRAUD. A representation that is contrary to the truth, made by a person who knows it is not true, for the purpose of inducing another to rely on the falsehood and to give up some property or other right.

157

GENERAL DAMAGES. Damages that are presumed by the law to arise from a particular wrongful act, because they are the direct and immediate result of the wrongful act. The difference between general and special damages is that general damages necessarily result from the wrongful act without regard to any special circumstances of the injured person.

GENERAL JURISDICTION COURTS. Courts that have jurisdiction to hear all types of cases.

GENERAL TRIAL CONFERENCE. This is simply one of many types of pretrial conferences that some courts conduct. Many courts will not have a general trial conference, but in their own efforts to conduct their business efficiently, most courts will have some type of pretrial conference.

INJUNCTION. A writ issued by a court ordering a defendant to do something or to refrain from doing, or continuing to do, something. An injunction can be issued by a court only if it determines that it would be fair and just to issue the injunction and that money damages alone would not be sufficient to protect the plaintiff.

INTERROGATORIES. Written questions directed to a witness that the witness is obligated to answer under oath.

JUDGMENT. As used in this book, judgment means the official decision of a court regarding the various rights and claims of the parties to a lawsuit. A judgment is issued only after a hearing of all the relevant evidence.

JUDGMENT NOTWITHSTANDING THE VERDICT. A judgment rendered by the judge in favor of one party notwithstanding the finding of a verdict in favor of the other party. Among lawyers, this is called a "Judgment NOV" from the Latin judgment non obstante veredicto.

JURISDICTION. The legal right by which judges exercise their authority. It exists when a court has the authority to recognize and decide a particular class of cases. In the United States, the jurisdiction of courts is determined by the various constitutions and legislatures.

LEGAL MATTERS. As used in this book, legal matters (as opposed to equitable matters) are those that are subject to being remedied by the payment of damages. In a different sense, legal matters (as opposed to factual matters) are those that are decided by the judge rather than by the jury.

159

MANDATORY SETTLEMENT CONFERENCE. This is another type of pretrial conference that some courts will have in order to force the parties to try to settle the lawsuit without the need for a trial.

MISDEMEANOR. Those crimes that are not as serious as felonies. Generally, those crimes that are not punishable by capital punishment or by imprisonment in a penitentiary for more than one year.

MISREPRESENTATION. An untrue statement of fact. An intentional misrepresentation is fraud. Negligent misrepresentation is a false representation made by a person who has no reasonable grounds for believing it to be true, even if he believes that it is true.

MITIGATE. As used in this book, to mitigate means to reduce the amount of damages that are owed. If you have suffered some injury and have mitigated your damages, you have taken efforts to cut your losses.

MOTION TO STRIKE. A motion made by a defendant to have all or portions of the plaintiff's complaint stricken as being sham or not supported by law.

160

MOTIONS. An application to the court for some ruling or order. A motion can be made in open court or by written application. Some motions will be made during trial and others before or after trial.

MOTIONS IN LIMINE. Motions made at the beginning of the trial. These are used to clear up evidence questions and to establish the procedures that will be used during the trial.

NEGLIGENCE. The failure to exercise that degree of care that a prudent person would exercise under the same circumstances. Negligence is characterized by conditions like inadvertence, thoughtlessness, inattention.

NONPERFORMANCE. The neglect, failure or refusal to do an act that you have agreed to do.

ORAL CONTRACT. An agreement that is not in writing or only partly in writing. An oral contract is enforceable, but enforcement depends upon the parties remembering what the words were that formed the basis for the agreement.

ORAL TESTIMONY. Evidence given by the words of a competent witness.

161

ORIGINAL JURISDICTION. The authority of a court to recognize a lawsuit at its beginning, to try it and to pass judgment on the law and the facts presented by it.

PEREMPTORY CHALLENGE. A challenge to the seating of a juror without having to state any cause or reason for the challenge.

PLAINTIFF. The person who starts a lawsuit.

PROMISSORY NOTE. A written promise to pay someone a certain amount of money at a certain time or at the time of that person's demand for payment.

PUNITIVE DAMAGES. Damages awarded to a plaintiff that are above and beyond damages necessary to compensate him for the wrong done to him. Punitive damages are awarded due to the violence, oppression, malice, fraud or wanton and wicked conduct of the defendant and are awarded for the purpose of punishing the defendant.

REAL PROPERTY. Land and the things attached to the land that are permanent, fixed and immovable.

REQUESTS FOR ADMISSIONS. A type of discovery in which one party asks another party to admit certain facts. The answering party must either admit or deny those facts under oath.

RULES OF LAW. Those rules which citizens must obey and follow or be subject to sanctions or legal consequences.

RULING. The decision of a court in connection with a motion or some objection to evidence.

SEIZURE. The forcible taking of property by a public officer. A seizure can occur following a judgment to enforce that judgment. As used in this book, seizure refers to taking possession of property in consequence of a violation of a public law.

SIDE BAR CONFERENCE. A meeting between the lawyers and the judge in the courtroom but out of hearing of the jury. These conferences are used for the lawyers to argue, and the judge to rule on, objections to evidence.

SPECIAL DAMAGES. Those damages that are the actual result of a wrongful act and which follow the wrongful act as a natural consequence of it. Special damages are distinguished from general damages in that special damages are not the necessary result of the wrongful act but rather the actual damages suffered by the particular injured party, even if other injured parties would not have suffered the same damages from the same wrongful act.

SPECIALTY COURTS. As used in this book, specialty courts are those courts that hear one type of case or a limited number of types of cases. Examples of specialty courts are courts that hear only probate matters and courts that hear only eviction cases.

SPECIFIC PERFORMANCE. The type of lawsuit by which one party seeks to force the other party to perform the terms of a contract. This type of lawsuit is often used in cases involving real property or in any other case in which money damages might not be adequate to compensate the injured party.

STATUS CONFERENCE. Yet another type of pretrial conference by which courts attempt to govern the progress of a case.

164

STATUTE OF FRAUDS. The name of an English statute passed in 1677 which has been adopted in some modified form in nearly every state. Statutes of frauds primarily provide that certain contracts cannot be enforced unless there is some writing to evidence the contract's existence. The writing must be signed by the party to be charged with enforcement of the contract or by his agent.

SUMMARY JUDGMENT. A judgment that follows a motion to have the case decided without a trial. Basically, a summary judgment says that there are no triable issues of fact and that the entire case can be disposed of by ruling only on the legal issues (as opposed to the factual issues) involved.

TRIAL BRIEF. A written document prepared by a lawyer in a lawsuit and filed with the court to inform it of the basic issues involved in the lawsuit and to present one parties arguments regarding various legal issues that are expected to arise during the trial.

TRIAL COURTS. Courts in which a lawsuit is initially filed and which conduct the trials of those lawsuits. Courts that have original jurisdiction.

TRIAL SETTING CONFERENCE. Still another type of pretrial conference that some courts conduct.

TRUST. There are many different types of trusts, but as used in this book, a trust is a right in property (either real property, personal property or both) held by one person for the benefit of another person. The person who holds property for the benefit of another is called the trustee; the one for whose benefit the property is held is called the beneficiary. The trustee has fiduciary duties to the beneficiary.

TRUST PROPERTY. The property that is held by one person for the benefit of another person. This property must be clearly identified and cannot be commingled with the property belonging to the trustee.

TRUSTEE. The person who holds property for the benefit of another in a trust relationship.

UNITED STATES DISTRICT COURTS. The trial courts operated by the federal government.

VERDICT. The decision by the jury, reported to the court, concerning the matters of fact that the jury was asked to deliberate on and decide in a lawsuit.

WRITS. As used in this book, a writ is an order by some court directing some lower court (or some administrative agency) to take some affirmative action or to rule differently. A writ is issued when the upper court determines that the lower court (or the administrative agency) did not correctly follow the law.

WRITTEN CONTRACT. An agreement the terms of which are in writing.

WRITTEN DOCUMENTS. The type of evidence that consists of written words as opposed to oral testimony. The document can be a formal document, memorandum or a hand written note.

ABOUT THE AUTHOR

Mr. Coombs is an attorney with over ten years of litigation experience. He was admitted to practice in California in 1976. Mr. Coombs' practice covers a wide range of real estate matters with particular emphasis in real estate acquisitions, title insurance, real estate title problems, the subdivision and development of real estate, mortgages and lender regulation. Mr. Coombs is currently chairman of the Client Relations Committee of the Orange County Bar Association.